Mike Barfield

Illustrated by Lauren Humphrey

THE ELEMENT IN THE ROOM

Investigating the Atomic Ingredients that Make Up Your Home

Laurence King Publishing

Your Mission: The case of the elusive elements

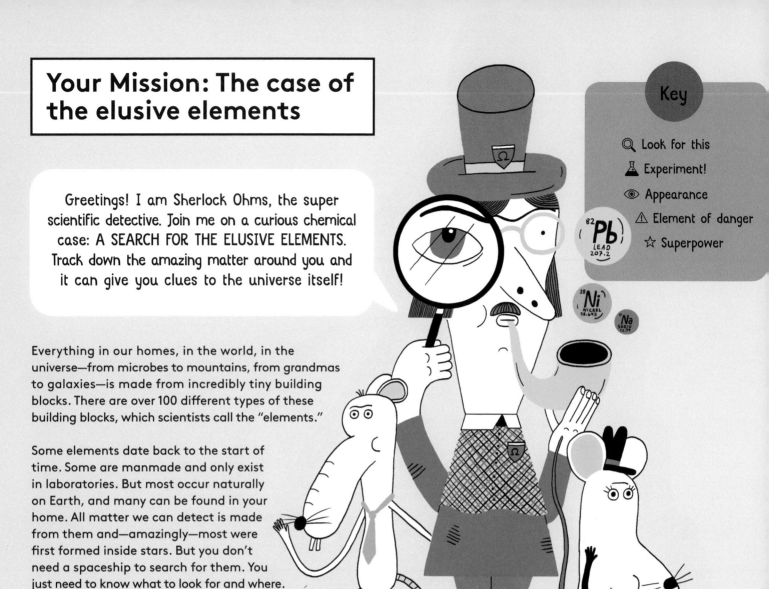

Greetings! I am Sherlock Ohms, the super scientific detective. Join me on a curious chemical case: A SEARCH FOR THE ELUSIVE ELEMENTS. Track down the amazing matter around you and it can give you clues to the universe itself!

Everything in our homes, in the world, in the universe—from microbes to mountains, from grandmas to galaxies—is made from incredibly tiny building blocks. There are over 100 different types of these building blocks, which scientists call the "elements."

Some elements date back to the start of time. Some are manmade and only exist in laboratories. But most occur naturally on Earth, and many can be found in your home. All matter we can detect is made from them and—amazingly—most were first formed inside stars. But you don't need a spaceship to search for them. You just need to know what to look for and where.

That's what this book is about. Along with my friends Ratley and Hattie, we will reveal what elements are, how they behave, and how YOU can detect them in your home. So join us on the hunt for... The Element in the Room!

Utterly elementary: atoms

The matter that makes up everything on Earth—air, water, cheese, *you*—is made from tiny particles called atoms. These are composed of even tinier particles known as protons, neutrons, and electrons. Each of the 118 known elements is a unique atom with a different number—from 1 to 118—of protons in its nucleus. That's what makes them elements! Elements are the building blocks of ordinary matter and can't be broken down into simpler substances by a chemical reaction. But their atoms can be "smashed" apart using powerful radiation!

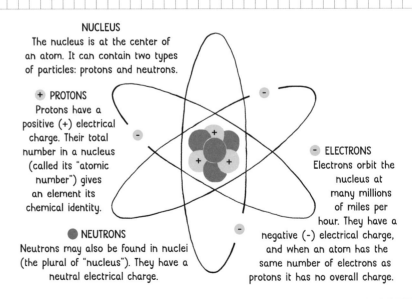

NUCLEUS
The nucleus is at the center of an atom. It can contain two types of particles: protons and neutrons.

+ PROTONS
Protons have a positive (+) electrical charge. Their total number in a nucleus (called its "atomic number") gives an element its chemical identity.

● NEUTRONS
Neutrons may also be found in nuclei (the plural of "nucleus"). They have a neutral electrical charge.

− ELECTRONS
Electrons orbit the nucleus at many millions of miles per hour. They have a negative (−) electrical charge, and when an atom has the same number of electrons as protons it has no overall charge.

🧪 The case of the hair-raising balloon

To demonstrate the effect of electrons for yourself, rub a blown-up balloon against your hair. Electrons are stripped from the atoms in your hair onto the balloon's surface. The extra electrons give the balloon a negative charge, which we call "static electricity." This negative charge will attract your hair and small pieces of paper to the balloon. And if the balloon has a high enough charge, it will even "stick" to a wall!

🧪 The case of the balloon lightning

Lightning is a giant discharge of static electricity caused by ice particles colliding inside clouds. You can make a similar mini-lightning bolt by rubbing a balloon with a cloth in the dark on a dry day and bringing it close to a metal object like a doorknob. A spark leaps between the two and the crackle you hear is a tiny thunderclap!

Tiny atoms

Atoms are unimaginably tiny! A teaspoon of sugar contains about 396 thousand million million million atoms of the elements carbon, hydrogen, and oxygen all combined together.

396,000,000,000,000,000,000,000

The empty atom

Amazingly, atoms are mostly empty space. Hold up a pin in the middle of a football field and ask a friend to run around its furthest edge. If the pin's head is taken to represent the size of a single proton in the nucleus of a hydrogen atom, then the orbiting electron would be a tiny speck of dust on your friend's nose. The distance between the two is just empty space, yet an element like gold can feel surprisingly solid!

Why did the balloon stick to the wall?

Elementary! Matching charges (+/+ or -/-) always repel. So the negative charge of the balloon repels the negative electrons in the atoms of the wall. This leaves the atoms of the wall with a positive charge from the remaining protons. Opposite charges (+/-) always attract, so the balloon sticks.

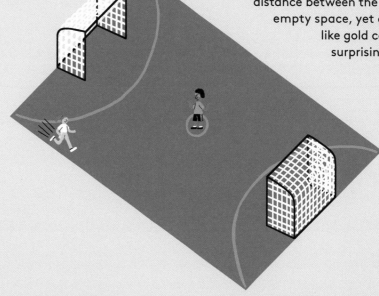

The First Mystery: The Big Bang

Our detective hunt begins 13.8 billion years ago! Back then, there was... nothing. No sun, no stars, no planets, no galaxies, no teachers, no homework, no elements, no matter, no clues. Then came the mind-blowing, monumental moment known as the Big Bang. This was when the universe was born, and it was the start of the incredible process that led to the elements being formed...

What existed before the Big Bang? No one knows. One theory says there was one infinitely hot, infinitely dense point known as a "singularity." Some also say there may be other universes!

1. INFLATION AND COOLING
From nothing, THE UNIVERSE EXPANDED and cooled in the minutest fraction of a second.

2. THE FIRST PARTICLES
A millionth of a second later, PROTONS AND NEUTRONS STARTED TO FORM.

3. THE FIRST ELEMENTS
Within two minutes, the nuclei of THE FIRST ELEMENT, HYDROGEN, BEGAN TO FORM. A MINUTE LATER, THE NUCLEI OF HELIUM FOLLOWED. After this, it took about 380,000 years for things to cool down enough for these nuclei to form stable atoms.

4. THE FIRST STARS
Clouds of hydrogen and helium were flung out across the newly formed universe. About 200 MILLION YEARS LATER, THE FORCE OF GRAVITY BEGAN TO FORM THEM INTO THE FIRST STARS. And these stars hold your first clue to the secrets of the elements.

How are elements formed in stars?
Elements are constantly being created in our universe. In the super-hot, super-dense centers of stars, the nuclei of hydrogen atoms are squeezed together. This nuclear reaction produces helium. It also creates visible light and other forms of radiation. That's what is happening in the center of our sun.

Larger stars
Larger stars continue fusing elements to produce heavier elements (with more protons), from oxygen all the way up to iron, before they also collapse and die. The reactions within them may also produce even heavier elements such as copper and zinc

Massive stars

Really massive stars—many times bigger than our sun—eventually collapse, producing a mega-explosion called a supernova. This can produce extra-heavy elements such as gold and uranium, which are then flung far into space.

Evidence of the Big Bang can still be discovered almost 14 billion years later. The radiation it released is visible in space as background microwaves, and can be detected by special radio telescopes.

The case of the disappearing sun

Our sun is vital for life on Earth but is actually quite a small star. Eventually it will run out of the elements that fuel fusion and will get colder and collapse, shedding its outer layer of heavier elements into space. But don't panic—it won't happen for about 5 billion years.

The mystery of the cosmic rays

Three lighter elements—lithium, beryllium, and boron—are thought to be made by "cosmic rays" splitting heavier elements in space into simpler atoms. Cosmic rays are high-energy particles whose origins are a mystery. They pose a serious health risk to space travelers, but rarely reach Earth's surface thanks to its atmosphere and magnetic field.

Xe Marks the Spot: Periodic Table

Every detective should draw up a list of suspects. Element detectives have a list of 118 to choose from, already arranged in a special table according to their weight and properties. Chemists call this the "Periodic Table."

The idea for the table originally came from a brilliant Russian nerd called Dmitri Mendeleev. And it was such a good idea that Mendeleev was able to use his table to predict the existence of elements that hadn't yet been discovered! However, the information the table contains today is the result of hundreds of years of detective work by lots of clever chemists, many of whom you will meet in our amazing Atomic Comics scattered throughout the book!

As you can see, the elements are arranged into rows and columns. The horizontal rows are known as "periods," giving the Periodic Table its name. The vertical columns are called "groups." Today's Periodic Table includes the 118 elements known so far, from hydrogen to oganesson, but could still acquire new members.

Each element has a chemical symbol, like a code name, which is made up of one or more letters. So Xe is the symbol for xenon.

Know your suspects

Like a map, the Periodic Table is full of information. Each element has a number at the top, which increases by one as you travel along each row from left to right. This is the element's "atomic number," and it tells you how many protons it has in its nucleus and is the key to an element's chemical identity. Hydrogen has one proton and therefore the atomic number 1. Helium has two protons and atomic number 2. As you travel along a row, the elements gain protons and become heavier. An electrically neutral atom has the same number of electrons as protons, so the table also reveals that a helium atom (atomic number 2) has two electrons orbiting its nucleus, and so on for all the other elements.

Also as in maps, elements in the table can be color-coded to indicate they have similarities. Most of the 118 elements are metals (like iron, Fe)—a large category which is then divided into several smaller groups. Then there are "non-metals," including the halogens and noble gases (like Xe, xenon). There are also some strange in-between elements called "metalloids." To make the table easier to show, two groups of metals called the lanthanides and actinides are usually placed in rows underneath the main table.

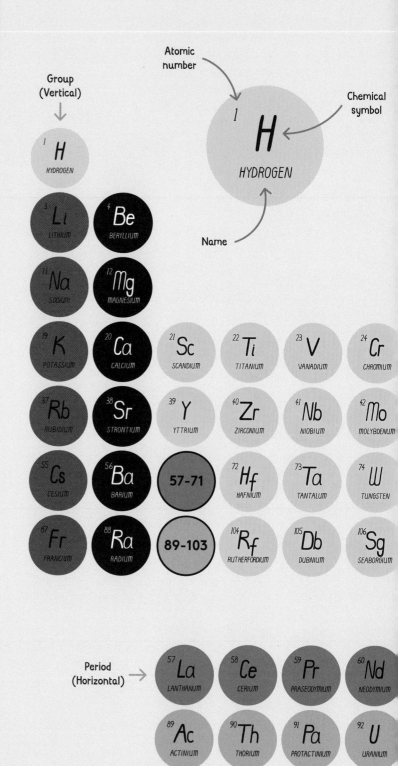

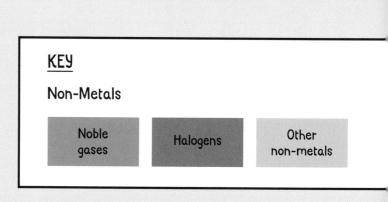

KEY

Non-Metals

| Noble gases | Halogens | Other non-metals |

Many elements are named after famous people and places. Mendelevium (Md) is named after Dmitri Mendeleev.

(1834–1907)

																	2 He HELIUM

5 B BORON	6 C CARBON	7 N NITROGEN	8 O OXYGEN	9 F FLUORINE	10 Ne NEON
13 Al ALUMINIUM	14 Si SILICON	15 P PHOSPHORUS	16 S SULFUR	17 Cl CHLORINE	18 Ar ARGON

25 Mn MANGANESE	26 Fe IRON	27 Co COBALT	28 Ni NICKEL	29 Cu COPPER	30 Zn ZINC	31 Ga GALLIUM	32 Ge GERMANIUM	33 As ARSENIC	34 Se SELENIUM	35 Br BROMINE	36 Kr KRYPTON
43 Tc TECHNETIUM	44 Ru RUTHENIUM	45 Rh RHODIUM	46 Pd PALLADIUM	47 Ag SILVER	48 Cd CADMIUM	49 In INDIUM	50 Sn TIN	51 Sb ANTIMONY	52 Te TELLURIUM	53 I IODINE	54 Xe XENON
75 Re RHENIUM	76 Os OSMIUM	77 Ir IRIDIUM	78 Pt PLATINUM	79 Au GOLD	80 Hg MERCURY	81 Tl THALLIUM	82 Pb LEAD	83 Bi BISMUTH	84 Po POLONIUM	85 At ASTATINE	86 Rn RADON
107 Bh BOHRIUM	108 Hs HASSIUM	109 Mt MEITNERIUM	110 Ds DARMSTADTIUM	111 Rg ROENTGENIUM	112 Cn COPERNICIUM	113 Nh NIHONIUM	114 Fl FLEROVIUM	115 Mc MOSCOVIUM	116 Lv LIVERMORIUM	117 Ts TENNESSINE	118 Og OGANESSON

61 Pm PROMETHIUM	62 Sm SAMARIUM	63 Eu EUROPIUM	64 Gd GADOLINIUM	65 Tb TERBIUM	66 Dy DYSPROSIUM	67 Ho HOLMIUM	68 Er ERBIUM	69 Tm THULIUM	70 Yb YTTERBIUM	71 Lu LUTETIUM
93 Np NEPTUNIUM	94 Pu PLUTONIUM	95 Am AMERICIUM	96 Cm CURIUM	97 Bk BERKELIUM	98 Cf CALIFORNIUM	99 Es EINSTEINIUM	100 Fm FERMIUM	101 Md MENDELEVIUM	102 No NOBELIUM	103 Lr LAWRENCIUM

Metals

Metalloids	Alkali metals	Alkaline earth metals	Lanthanides	Actinides	Transition metals	Post-transition metals

Identity Parade: Masters of Disguise

Although some elements (like gold, Au) can be found on Earth in their simplest form, many are in disguise. Their atoms join up in set ways with the atoms of one or more other elements to form "gangs" called molecules.

New substances formed from these molecules can often have very different properties to their component elements. As a result, chemists often have to carry out some clever detective work to identify them!

State secrets!

Appearances can be deceptive! Matter in your home can exist in one of three main states—solid, liquid or gas. And some substances can be found in all three disguises. Cunning!

IN A STATE
Water can be found in the room in all three states depending on the temperature: ice in the freezer, water in the bath, steam from a kettle!

All about sharing

The bonds between the different atoms in a molecule are formed by sharing electrons. An electrically neutral atom has the same number of electrons orbiting its nucleus as its atomic number. Scientists think of these electrons as occupying concentric shells around the nucleus, like the layers of an onion. The shell closest to the nucleus can hold up to two electrons. The next two shells can each have eight, with the numbers increasing as atoms increase in size.

An atom with a "full" outermost electron shell is less chemically reactive than one with a part-empty shell. In molecules, atoms share electrons to become more stable.

This is an argon (Ar) atom. Its outermost electron shell is full. As a result, argon is so chemically inert that no natural argon compounds exist.

In a SOLID, such as a lump of metal, the molecules are closely packed in fixed positions and bonded to their neighbors. They vibrate but can't move about, so solids have a set shape and volume.

In a LIQUID, such as water, the bonds between molecules are weaker and the molecules move around more. Liquids have a set volume but take the shape of the container they are in.

In a GAS, the molecules escape their bonds and can move about freely, with no fixed volume or shape.

The state of a substance depends on its temperature and the pressure it is under. Gases become liquids if you squash their molecules together, and solids will melt if you heat them enough. In this book, all our elements are described in the state they would take in a home at room temperature and close to sea level.

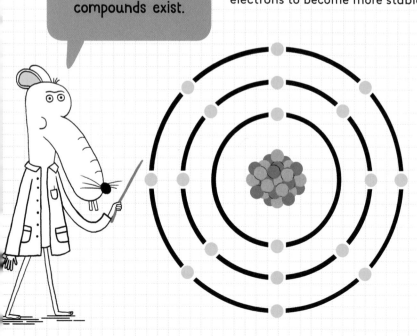

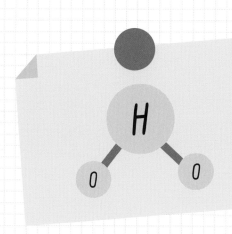

In the mix

Different chemicals can also be combined together in what chemists call a "mixture." Unlike a compound, the components of a mixture are not bonded together and can be separated without resorting to chemical reactions. For example, dissolving sugar in hot water produces a sugar–water mixture. Pour the mixture onto a plate and the water will eventually evaporate away, leaving behind unchanged sugar crystals.

Code name compound

When atoms of more than one element join together chemically the resulting substance is called a compound. Water is a compound formed from the elements hydrogen (H) and oxygen (O). A water molecule always contains two hydrogen atoms and one oxygen atom, giving it the chemical formula H_2O. These "code names" are clues to the make-up of molecules and how they will behave chemically. Here are some more common household molecules:

methane (CH_4)
carbon dioxide (CO_2)
ammonia (NH_3)

Some elements also form molecules made solely of their own atoms. Oxygen in the air has the molecular form O_2. Oxygen atoms share electrons to form more stable molecules.

O — O

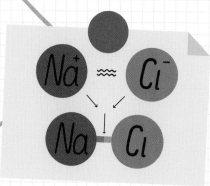

ID: ion

Ions are atoms or molecules that have an overall electrical charge. They become positively charged (+) by losing electrons and negatively charged (-) by gaining electrons.

Bonds formed between oppositely charged ions are some of the strongest in chemistry. Table salt is mostly sodium chloride (NaCl). Its molecules have an ionic bond between a positively charged sodium ion (Na+) and a negatively charged chlorine ion (Cl-). The two charges attract and cancel each other out.

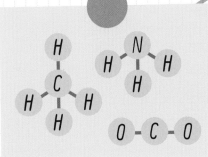

Agent alloy

An alloy is a special form of mixture, often involving a metal. Steel is an alloy of iron (Fe) and carbon (C) that is both harder and stronger than pure iron. Brass is an alloy of copper (Cu) and zinc (Zn).

SUSPECTS 1 TO 92
Periodic Tables at a glance: 92 elements occur naturally; another 26 can be found in laboratories. Along with a little help from Hattie and Ratley, it is time to crack the case of... The Element in the Room!

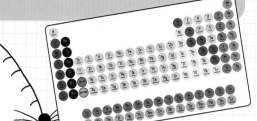

Hydrogen

◉ Colorless, odorless gas
⚠ Highly flammable ☆ Invisibility

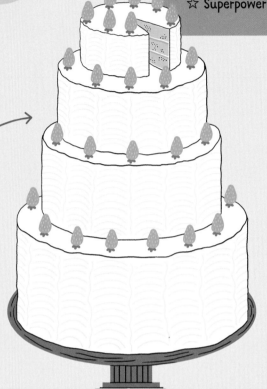

Hydrogen makes up almost three-quarters of the total mass of elements in the universe. If you could count all the different atoms in the universe, over 90% of them would be hydrogen atoms. You won't be able to spot them, because hydrogen is an invisible, odorless gas. But you can track them down in millions of different substances.

Hydrogen is a highly reactive element, which means it forms lots of compounds with other elements. These include natural substances such as fats, oils, sugars and starches, so you can have fun finding hydrogen by eating it in your food!

You will also find hydrogen atoms in yourself: they are in proteins and bodily fluids, and make up almost 10% of the weight of your body.

Remember...

◉ Appearance
⚠ Element of danger
☆ Superpower

¹ H

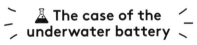

🧪 The case of the underwater battery

You can use electricity to release the hydrogen atoms from water molecules. Chemists call this "electrolysis." Submerge a 9-volt battery upright in a glass of cold water. Small bubbles of hydrogen gas form at the negative terminal (marked "-") and rise to the surface. Ask an adult to hold a lit match to the bubbles, and they will ignite. Make sure to take the battery out and dry it off afterwards, or it will quickly go dead.

Two's company
Hydrogen atoms are the simplest of any element, with a single proton in the nucleus and a single orbiting electron. But when it's a gas, the atoms gang up in pairs to form hydrogen molecules (H_2) as these make them more stable.

I'm H_2.

And I'm H_2 too!

FIND IT IN:

- [ ] YOU
- [ ] WATER
- [ ] EVERYTHING THAT CONTAINS WATER
- [ ] FOOD
- [ ] FARTS
- [ ] BATTERIES
- [ ] THE SUN

Follow the scent

Harmless bacteria in our intestines produce a mixture of gases that come out when we fart (everybody does it!). This mixture includes some smelly gases, as well as nitrogen (the major component of air) and even a big hunk of hydrogen. This means some farts can literally be explosive!

Code name "water former"

When hydrogen burns in air, water is produced. Early chemists spotted this, and hydrogen's name means "water former" in Greek. Water is a compound with the formula H_2O, meaning that a water molecule has two atoms of hydrogen (H_2) for every single atom of oxygen (O). So, if you have a thirst to find the element in the room, you can gulp down billions of atoms in a single glass of water!

What a gas!

Scientists estimate that there are about one quinvigintillion atoms in the universe. That's a 1 followed by 78 zeros. Or if you prefer, one million million million million million million million million million million million million million atoms. Either way, it's a huge number, and nine in every ten are hydrogen atoms!

Luckily the universe is big enough to fit them all in!

1,000,000,000,000,000,
000,000,000,000,000,
000,000,000,000,
000,000,000,
000,000,000,
000,000,000,
000,000,000,
000,000,000

000,
000,
000,
000

Helium

2 He

👁 Colorless, odorless, tasteless gas
⚠ None ☆ High-flying

Helium is the second most abundant element in the universe after hydrogen. Despite being really light, it makes up almost a quarter of the total mass of all the elements put together. But on Earth it is so rare that some scientists think we may soon run out—and then we'll need to mine it from the surface of the moon.

Helium is the only element to have been discovered in space before it was found on Earth. French astronomer Jules Janssen was studying a solar eclipse in 1868 when he noticed a bright-yellow band in the light coming from the sun, which he couldn't match with any other known element. The light turned out to be given off by helium, which takes its name from *helios*, the Greek word for "sun."

Helium becomes a liquid at very low temperatures or when stored under great pressure (such as in the metal cylinders used for filling balloons). Liquid helium can be used to keep things very cold: the fuel tanks of space rockets, hospital scanners, supercomputers, and the Large Hadron Collider.

🧪 The case of the squeaky voice

Making sure an adult is around, take a party balloon filled with helium and gulp in a small mouthful of the gas. When you try to speak, your voice will sound squeaky. This is because sound travels faster through helium than through air.

The effect is safe (and very funny!), but make sure you take a proper breath of air afterwards.

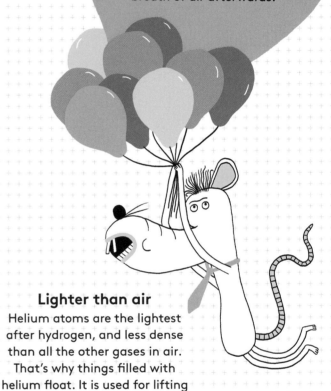

Lighter than air
Helium atoms are the lightest after hydrogen, and less dense than all the other gases in air. That's why things filled with helium float. It is used for lifting airships and weather balloons into the air. To track it down, just head for a party and you will find it inside floating party balloons.

Why do party balloons stop floating?
Elementary! The helium atoms are so small that they escape through the gaps between the molecules of rubber that make up the balloon. More expensive silvery plastic balloons should stay afloat longer, because they have molecules that are closer together.

FIND IT IN:
☐ PARTY BALLOONS
☐ SMOKE ALARMS
☐ HOSPITAL SCANNERS
☐ SUPERCOMPUTERS
☐ THE SUN

Lithium

3 Li

👁 Soft silver-white metal
⚠ Highly reactive ☆ Super battery

Lithium is the lightest metal in the universe, and the least dense solid element. It is so light that it floats on water—but it also reacts with water, giving off flammable hydrogen gas. In fact, lithium is so reactive it must be stored in oil away from moisture and air.

Some lithium was made in the Big Bang, and more has been made by the action of cosmic rays. But scientists think there is less lithium in the universe than there should be. Where has it gone? It's a mystery!

FIND IT IN:
☐ BATTERIES
☐ FIREWORKS
☐ MEDICINES

🔍 The case of the hidden code

To find out if the watch battery in one of your electronic devices contains lithium, you need to look for the secret code. If you can find a code written on a battery with a "C" in it—such as CR2032—then there's lithium in it. (The "R" just tells you the battery is round!)

Red rocket
You can track lithium down in flares and rockets. If they burn with a bright-red color, they may well contain lithium compounds.

Battery farm
Most of the world's lithium goes into making the batteries used in portable electronic devices. These include tablets, mobile phones, and laptops, so you shouldn't struggle to track it down!

ATOMIC COMICS

THE GREEK DETECTIVES: THE CASE OF THE FOUR ELEMENTS

1

THE CONCEPT OF "ATOMS" GOES BACK TO THE ANCIENT GREEKS.

Ancient? I'm only 25!

Lucky you.

(5TH CENTURY BCE)

THE IDEA IS ATTRIBUTED TO PHILOSOPHER LEUCIPPUS OF MILETUS AND HIS PUPIL DEMOCRITUS...

Done your chemistry homework, Democritus?

Er, the dog ate it...

HOWEVER, IT'S POSSIBLE THAT LEUCIPPUS DIDN'T ACTUALLY EXIST.

HOORAY!

P'NG

DEMOCRITUS ARGUED THAT IF YOU CUT SOMETHING INTO INCREASINGLY SMALLER PIECES...

Greek salad, anyone?

...EVENTUALLY THE PIECES COULD GET NO SMALLER. HE CALLED THESE FINAL PIECES "ATOMS."

Er, atom salad, anyone?

THE WORD "ATOM" IS GREEK FOR "UNCUTTABLE" OR "INDIVISIBLE."

"Inedible," more like.

DEMOCRITUS THOUGHT ATOMS HAD DIFFERENT SIZES (CORRECT!) AND DIFFERENT SHAPES (WRONG!)...

IRON

Iron atoms have hooks that lock them into a solid.

BUT HE WAS RIGHT ABOUT SOME THINGS...

There are gaps between atoms which I call a void.

BUT NOT EVERYONE AGREED, INCLUDING GREEK SUPER-GEEK ARISTOTLE...

The real void is in here.

INSTEAD, ARISTOTLE BELIEVED THERE WERE JUST FOUR ELEMENTS – EARTH, AIR, FIRE, AND WATER – EACH WITH THEIR OWN UNIQUE SHAPE.

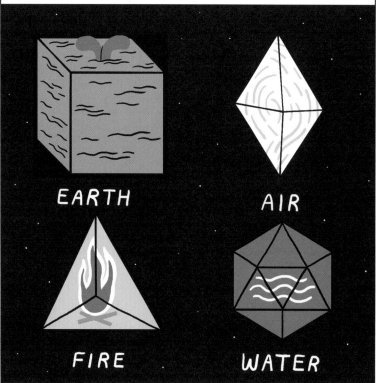

EARTH

AIR

FIRE

WATER

ARISTOTLE CLAIMED THAT ALL MATTER WAS MADE FROM THESE...

Your water, sir.

BUT ACTUALLY DEMOCRITUS WAS CLOSER TO THE TRUTH...

Your hydrogen and oxygen atoms, sir.

Beryllium

⁴ **Be**

👁 Light, silvery metal
⚠ Don't inhale ☆ X-ray vision

Beryllium is a rare metal element only found naturally in certain minerals in the ground. A beryllium compound called beryl forms beautiful aquamarine (pale blue) and emerald (deep green) gemstones.

FIND IT IN:

☐ GEMSTONES
☐ X-RAY MACHINES
☐ SATELLITES
☐ TOOLS

Alloy there!
Beryllium is often added to other metals to make alloys. Mixed with copper it is used in super-safe tools that don't generate sparks if they hit steel surfaces (useful when working near explosive chemicals!). Because beryllium metals are light, they are also used in aircraft, guided missiles, and satellites.

The Bahia Emerald, one of the largest in the world, has been valued at $400 million.

BAHIA EMERALD 2001

X-ray specks
Inhaling dust from beryllium and its compounds can cause a serious lung condition called berylliosis. But beryllium also plays an important part in healthcare. Because its atoms are so small, beryllium metal is transparent to X-rays—they just pass straight through it. So you will discover this element in X-ray machines!

Boron

⁵ **B**

👁 Black-brown metalloid
⚠ Essential ☆ Shape changer

Boron is vital for life. It helps to keep our bones strong and healthy, and can be found in foods including beans, bananas, and broccoli—all beginning with its code name B! Lots of washing powders and cleaning products (such as borax) also contain boron compounds.

FIND IT IN:

☐ BEANS
☐ BANANAS
☐ BROCCOLI
☐ CLEANING PRODUCTS
☐ CRASH HELMETS
☐ SURFBOARDS
☐ SILLY PUTTY

Pyrex marks the spot
Boron is combined with silicon to make borosilicate glass, which won't crack during sudden changes in temperature. This makes it perfect for laboratory test tubes and Pyrex cookware.

Boron is used in fiberglass, a kind of plastic mixed with glass fibers that provide extra strength. This can be molded into amazing shapes and is used to make everything from cars to crash helmets, surfboards to ships.

⚗ The case of the boron-based slime
Make your own Silly Putty by dissolving a spoonful of borax in a cup with a small amount of cold water. Add a dollop of white PVA glue and mix together. It should form a slimy ball that can be squished like a liquid, but also bounce and be torn in half! The boron atoms in the borax link the long chains of molecules (called polymers) in the glue to turn them into super-slime. (Keep it covered in the fridge.)

Carbon

👁 Often dark, sometimes shiny
⚠ Possible planetary menace!
☆ Master of disguise

Carbon is common! It's the second most common element in the human body after oxygen. It's the fourth most common element by mass in the universe. It's the fifteenth most common element in the Earth's crust. And yet carbon is also super-special—it is essential to all known life.

Carbon atoms are very versatile in the bonds they can form with other elements. There are over 10 million carbon compounds, and the study of these is called organic chemistry. Carbon is found in every living thing—including us. It's also in the things we eat, drink, wear, and use. Everything made of plastic contains carbon.

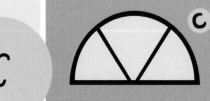

6
C

C

🔍 Carbon copy
To get on the trail of carbon, just look at the pages of this book and the ink printed on them: they both contain carbon.

C

C

FIND IT IN:

- ☐ YOU
- ☐ PETS
- ☐ FOOD
- ☐ TOAST
- ☐ SUGARY DRINKS
- ☐ PLANTS
- ☐ COAL
- ☐ CHARCOAL
- ☐ OIL
- ☐ GASOLINE
- ☐ CLOTHES
- ☐ PLASTICS
- ☐ RUBBER
- ☐ THIS BOOK
- ☐ PENCILS

Global warming
Coal, the fossilized remains of plants that died over 250 million years ago in the Carboniferous Period, is full of carbon. Billions of tons of coal are mined every year and burned to generate electricity. This produces carbon dioxide, a "greenhouse gas," which contributes to global warming. That's why we are trying to find cleaner forms of energy than carbon-rich fossil fuels such as coal, gas, and oil.

🔍 2B or not 2B
Make a sketch of your suspect, and you will be sure to track down carbon: it is contained in the pencil you are using! The "lead" in pencils is not actually made from the element lead, but rather from graphite, an allotrope of carbon. In graphite, carbon atoms are arranged in weakly bonded layers that slide over each other to leave a mark when rubbed on paper.

🧪 The case of the electric pencil
Graphite is highly unusual for a non-metal, as it will conduct electricity. Ask an adult to help you split open a pencil to reveal the "lead" inside. Then, make a simple circuit with a bulb and a battery (*see diagram*). Complete the circuit by touching the wires to the pencil "lead," and the bulb should light up.

It's a steel

Adding a small percentage of carbon to steel makes it stronger and harder. Carbon steel is used to build bridges, houses, washing machines, and fridges. Adding even more carbon creates cast iron. This is a brittle but strong metal, and you can track it down in railings, manhole covers, pots, and pans.

Master of disguise

Carbon is a master of disguise. It can arrange its atoms in different ways to produce different materials, known as allotropes, all of which are still "pure" carbon. Some occur naturally, others are manmade. Allotropes of carbon include diamonds, coal, graphite, charcoal, and graphene.

🧪 The case of the lemon fire extinguisher

Carbon dioxide is a compound of one atom of carbon (C) and two atoms of oxygen (O_2), with the code name CO_2. It is the gas that makes drinks fizzy and is also used in some fire extinguishers.

You can produce your own carbon dioxide by mixing some bicarbonate of soda or baking powder with lemon juice in a cup or glass. The chemical reaction gives off CO_2, which is heavier than air. If you very gently tilt the cup or glass over a lit candle, the flame should go out.

WARNING!
Get an adult to help, and don't touch the flame.

·Pets
·Food
·Clothes
·Plants
·coal

BAKING POWDER
100g

Nitrogen

^{7}N

👁 Colorless, odorless gas
⚠ Explosive compounds! ☆ Super noisy

You don't need to look for nitrogen, nitrogen finds you! That's because, although you can't see or taste it, nitrogen gas makes up 78% of the air we breathe. And because our bodies can't absorb it from the air, every lungful—in and out—is largely nitrogen.

Nitrogen atoms are in the DNA molecules of genes—the basic blueprints of living things—and in the amino acids that make up the proteins (muscles and tissues) of our bodies. These constantly need replacing, so we should eat about 3 ounces (80) of eggs, meat, fish or nuts every day.

FIND IT IN:

☐ YOU
☐ CHRISTMAS CRACKERS
☐ AIR
☐ POOP
☐ PEE
☐ EGGS
☐ FISH
☐ MEAT
☐ BEANS
☐ APPLE SEEDS
☐ NYLON CLOTHING

🔍 The case of the Christmas cracker

Compounds containing nitrogen can be scarily reactive. It is found in unstable explosives such as gunpowder, nitroglycerin, and TNT, and at home in Christmas crackers. Take one apart and find the explosive compound (silver fulminate, AgCNO) on the cardboard strip. Hit it with a hammer and it will go "BANG!"

What a waste

Urine is 94% water (H_2O), with the rest being soluble compounds from our bodies. Compounds containing nitrogen give human waste its color. Urobilin makes urine yellow and stercobilin makes poop brown. The nitrogen in human waste was once valuable: poop was collected as fertilizer for crops and pee was used to make gunpowder!

🔍 The case of the sinister seed

Cyanides are a group of highly poisonous chemicals containing carbon and nitrogen atoms linked together. Cut open an apple and remove the seeds. These contain a natural sugar that releases a tiny amount of cyanide in your stomach if you swallow them. It's far too little to hurt you, but it's best to spit them out anyway.

What a gas

Nitrogen forms lots of compounds with oxygen. Nitrous oxide (N_2O) is often called "laughing gas," as it can make people giggle when inhaled.

Oxygen

^{8}O

◉ Colorless, odorless gas
⚠ Feeds flames! ☆ Essential for life

Oxygen is the most common element on Earth and the third most abundant in the universe. Oxygen makes up about a fifth (21%) of the air we breathe and almost two-thirds (65%) of our bodies are oxygen, thanks to humans being mostly made of water (H_2O).

When the Earth was formed over 4 billion years ago its atmosphere contained almost no oxygen. As simple life forms evolved they began producing O_2 as a waste product. Slowly it built up in the atmosphere, and today without oxygen almost every living thing on Earth would die.

Oxygen is also essential for combustion—without it, we couldn't light fires, heat our homes or operate cars, planes, and machines.

⚗ The case of the breathing weed

In sunlight, green plants combine water from the soil with carbon dioxide in the air to produce sugar and oxygen in a process called "photosynthesis." The plants release the oxygen through their leaves.

To track down oxygen, submerge some spinach in a glass of water. Leave it in strong sunlight, and photosynthesis will produce small bubbles of oxygen on the leaves.

Why is oxygen everywhere?

Elementary! Because it is very reactive and forms millions of compounds called "oxides." Oxygen atoms are found in everything from glass to grass, from dust to rust (ferric oxide), and in almost all our food and drink. A glass of orange juice has oxygen atoms in the glass itself, in the water molecules that make up most of the juice, in the acids and sugars from the fruit, and in dissolved oxygen from the air.

FIND IT IN:

☐ YOU
☐ AIR
☐ WATER
☐ TEA
☐ COFFEE
☐ CHOCOLATE
☐ SUGAR
☐ GLASS
☐ LEMON JUICE
☐ ORANGE JUICE
☐ PLANTS
☐ RUST

⚗ The case of the cold bubbles

Many gases, including oxygen, dissolve in water. Fish breathe this dissolved oxygen by passing water over their gills. The amount of oxygen that dissolves can depend on its temperature. Cover two glasses of cold water with plastic wrap. Put one in the fridge and the other in a warm, sunny place. The next day, you should see bubbles only in the warm glass. This is oxygen that has come out of solution, showing that warmer water holds less oxygen. This is bad news for our oceans—if they warm up due to climate change then the creatures that live there will be affected.

I'm preparing for the worst...

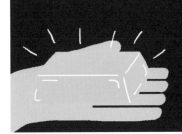

FOR THOUSANDS OF YEARS, PEOPLE TRIED TO TURN LESS VALUABLE SUBSTANCES INTO GOLD... WITHOUT SUCCESS!

Gold?

No. Just old.

(THE MIDDLE AGES)

THESE EARLY CHEMISTS WERE CALLED ~~IDIOTS~~ ALCHEMISTS, WITH THE WORD "ALCHEMY" GOING BACK TO ANCIENT EGYPT.

Are you a mummy?

No, my experiment exploded. GROAN.

(1900 BCE)

ALCHEMISTS OFTEN WORKED IN SECRET AS MANY OF THEIR BELIEFS BORDERED ON BLACK MAGIC.

Is this magic?

BOOM

WELL, it's made our eyebrows disappear.

ALCHEMISTS ALSO SEARCHED FOR A "UNIVERSAL PANACEA" (PAN-AH-SEE-AH) CAPABLE OF CURING ALL DISEASES AND PROLONGING YOUTH.

I'LL find the secret of eternal life, even if it kills me...

ALCHEMY RECOGNIZED 16 NATURAL ELEMENTS, OF WHICH GOLD WAS THE PUREST AND MOST PERFECT.

AS GOOD AS GOLD

NOT AS GOOD AS GOLD

LUMP OF LEAD

THESE ELEMENTS (SEE BOX ON RIGHT) WERE EACH GIVEN SECRET SYMBOLS SO ALCHEMISTS COULD RECORD THEIR RESULTS. SOME WERE QUITE BAFFLING.

What is it?*

I dunno.

*THE SYMBOL FOR ANTIMONY (SEE PAGE 45).

MANY OF THE ELEMENTS HAD SYMBOLS THAT LINKED THEM TO OBJECTS IN THE HEAVENS WITH THE SUN BEING THE SYMBOL FOR GOLD (OF COURSE).

Just working on my "gold"-tan.

BESIDES ELEMENTS, ALCHEMISTS HAD SECRET SYMBOLS FOR EVERYTHING ELSE THEY USED TOO.

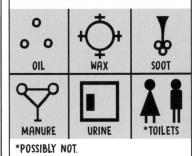

OIL	WAX	SOOT
MANURE	URINE	*TOILETS

*POSSIBLY NOT.

MANY EUROPEAN ALCHEMISTS SEARCHED FOR "THE PHILOSOPHER'S STONE," BELIEVING IT WOULD GRANT ETERNAL LIFE – THE SAME STONE MENTIONED IN THE HARRY POTTER BOOKS!

Philosopher's Stone?

Got it on DVD...

EARLY ALCHEMY SLOWLY LED TO MODERN CHEMISTRY. THE GERMAN MONK ALBERTUS MAGNUS ISOLATED ARSENIC IN ABOUT 1250CE – THE FIRST ELEMENT WITH A KNOWN DISCOVERER.

No, it's NOT named after me.

ARSENIC

BUT IF YOU THINK WE'VE LEFT ALCHEMY FAR BEHIND US, THINK AGAIN. THE VOLVO CARS LOGO IS THE OLD ALCHEMICAL SYMBOL FOR IRON!

I bought it with all the gold I made!

Fluorine

9 F

👁 Pale-yellow gas
⚠ Extremely reactive ☆ Serious bite

Fluorine is rare, which may be a good thing given how fiercely reactive it is. It reacts with almost every element, even including some noble gases.

Fluorine reacts with water to form hydrofluoric acid, an acid so strong it can burn through glass. Many chemists who tried to isolate fluorine as an element suffered terrible accidents, losing eyes, limbs, and their lives. They are known as the "fluorine martyrs."

FIND IT IN:

☐ FLUORIDE TOOTHPASTE

☐ TEA

☐ NON-STICK (TEFLON) SAUCEPANS

☐ BREATHABLE (GORE-TEX) WATERPROOF CLOTHING

Smile please
Tooth enamel is the hardest substance in the body, but it still gets destroyed by the acids produced when the bacteria in our mouths break down sugars. That's why we need to brush twice a day. The fluorine atoms in fluoride toothpaste bond with our tooth enamel to make it even harder and more resistant to decay.

Neon

10 Ne

👁 Colorless, odorless, tasteless gas ⚠ None, it's inert ☆ Glows in the dark

Look at the Periodic Table, and you will find neon among the noble gases, which are all very unreactive. Its name means "new," which neon was in 1898 when it was first discovered! It is so light that it can float up and escape from the Earth's atmosphere.

If you pass electricity through neon it produces an orangey-red glow. So if you track down an old advertising sign, it might contain neon. Painting the glass turns neon signs different colors.

10 Ne-on

FIND IT IN:

☐ AIR

☐ NEON SIGNS

☐ OLD CD PLAYERS

See the light
Helium-neon (He-Ne) lasers, which produce a red light, were fitted in early CD players. These have mostly been replaced by cheaper diode lasers, but your parents might still have one.

¹¹Na Sodium

◉ Soft silvery metal
⚠ Don't get it wet! ☆ Ice-melter

Sodium allows nerves in our bodies to send signals and helps regulate our blood pressure. Lucky then that it is so easily available on Earth—not as the elemental metal (pure sodium is so reactive that it explodes in contact with water!), but in many common compounds.

One very familiar sodium compound is sodium chloride (NaCl), which we know as table salt. This is mined from huge underground deposits—the dried-up remains of prehistoric seas, many of which formed over 200 million years ago.

FIND IT IN:

☐ YOU
☐ URINE
☐ TABLE SALT
☐ BICARBONATE OF SODA
☐ FOOD ADDITIVES
☐ WINDOWS
☐ BOTTLES
☐ JARS
☐ SEA WATER

Why is rock salt sprinkled on roads?

Elementary! Water that has salt dissolved in it needs a lower temperature to freeze. So the salted ice melts, making the roads safer.

We should be careful how much salt we consume, as too much can cause health problems.

Our bodies balance the sodium in our tissues. Excess sodium is removed by our kidneys and carried away in our urine.

— ⚗ The case of the magic cube —

Float an ice cube in a glass of cold water and try to pick it up with the end of a piece of string. Impossible! Now lay the wet end of the string on the ice cube and sprinkle salt over it. Leave for a few seconds, then gently pull the string. The ice cube should rise! (The salt briefly melts the water on top of the ice cube. It then refreezes, sticking the string to the cube.)

— ⚗ The case of the white crystals —

At the seaside, gather a jar of water from a clean bit of sea water, away from any pollution. Back at home, pour it into a bowl and leave in a warm place and the water will slowly evaporate to leave behind white crystals. These will mostly be sodium chloride but may also include salts of other metals such as potassium, magnesium, and calcium.

Magnesium

12 Mg

◉ Shiny gray metal
⚠ Burns in air ☆ Photosynthesis

Magnesium is essential for life. The chlorophyll molecule found in the leaves of green plants has magnesium at its center and is a vital part of the photosynthesis process. Photosynthesis gives us oxygen in the air and is the origin of almost everything we eat.

Magnesium is also present in every cell type of every organism, especially in bones and muscles. It helps cells release energy. To keep our bodies healthy, we should eat magnesium-rich foods such as dark chocolate, seeds, and nuts—and lots of leafy green vegetables.

Alloy there!

Magnesium is combined with other metals to make alloys that are both hard and lightweight. Alloyed with aluminum it is used in car wheels, cameras, laptops, mobile phones, golf clubs, aircraft, archery bows, power tools, and bicycles. Racing bikes can have frames of pure magnesium.

FIND IT IN:

- ☐ YOU
- ☐ GREEN PLANTS
- ☐ LEAFY VEGETABLES
- ☐ BRAZIL NUTS
- ☐ ALMONDS
- ☐ PUMPKIN SEEDS
- ☐ DARK CHOCOLATE
- ☐ MINERAL WATERS
- ☐ LAPTOPS
- ☐ MOBILE PHONES
- ☐ GOLF CLUBS
- ☐ BIKE FRAMES
- ☐ SPARKLERS

Magnesium is light and burns in air with a bright-white flame. It puts the spark into sparklers!

🔍 **In the drink**

Mineral waters often contain magnesium, leached from rocks in the Earth's crust. A distinctive taste can help you detect magnesium, but also look for clues on the label.

Aluminum

^{13} Al

👁 Light, silvery-white metal
⚠ Mostly harmless ☆ Eternal recycler

Aluminum appears on Earth in the form of compounds in rocks, though the molten pure metal may exist inside some active volcanoes. It is incredibly versatile and can be found all around our homes. The recycling bin is a good place to start.

Aluminum is highly malleable, which means it can be pulled and squashed into different shapes, including a thin foil that is safe to wrap around food. As it keeps out light and air, aluminum foil is good for keeping chocolate fresh. But be careful not to leave foil on your food if you have metal fillings in your teeth: the foil and fillings can react with the spit in your mouth to produce a tiny electric shock!

🔍 The case of the failed magnet

Food and drink cans are made either from steel (a form of iron) or aluminum. Both can be recycled and YOU can sort them the same way they do at the recycling center. Take a fridge magnet and see if it sticks to the side of the can. Make two piles. Aluminum is non-magnetic, so only the steel cans will have been attracted to the magnet. Sorted!

Fe

Aluminum jewels
Large crystals of aluminum oxide (Al_2O_3) occur in nature, and traces of other elements turn these crystals beautiful colors including red (rubies), blue (sapphires), green, and yellow.

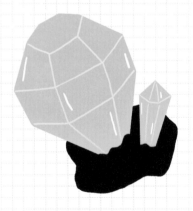

It's etern-Al
Aluminum is infinitely renewable. Anything made of aluminum can be melted down and made into new things without any loss of quality, forever! The aluminum can was first introduced in the USA in 1959. When you drink from one today it may contain the same aluminum your great-grandparents drank from!

1959 1959 1959 1959 1959 1959 1959 1959 1959

🔬 The case of the boiled foil

Pure aluminum reacts with oxygen in the air to form a coating of aluminum oxide. This protects the rest of the metal from further chemical change.

You can make your own aluminum oxide by carefully boiling aluminum foil in water (ask an adult to help you). Boil a square until the foil darkens and turns black or brown. This coating is aluminum oxide. When everything has cooled, scrape it off carefully with scissors to show the bright metal beneath.

FIND IT IN:

- ☐ CDS
- ☐ DVDS
- ☐ BLU-RAYS
- ☐ COMPUTERS
- ☐ MOBILE PHONES
- ☐ WINDOW FRAMES
- ☐ KITCHEN FOIL
- ☐ FOOD AND DRINK CANS
- ☐ SAUCEPANS
- ☐ SILVER PAINT
- ☐ MIRRORS
- ☐ TOOTHPASTE
- ☐ SUNSCREEN
- ☐ BIKE FRAMES
- ☐ POWDER INSIDE AN ETCH A SKETCH

As good as gold

Aluminum was first isolated in tiny quantities in 1825. At the time, it was so rare and expensive that the French emperor Napoleon III ate off aluminum plates rather than gold ones. Just think of that next time you're sitting round the campfire boiling the aluminum camping kettle!

Hot properties

Aluminum powder mixed with several other chemicals burns at an incredibly high temperature. Known as thermite, it is used to weld railway tracks together. It can get as hot as 2,500°C—the same as some stars in outer space!

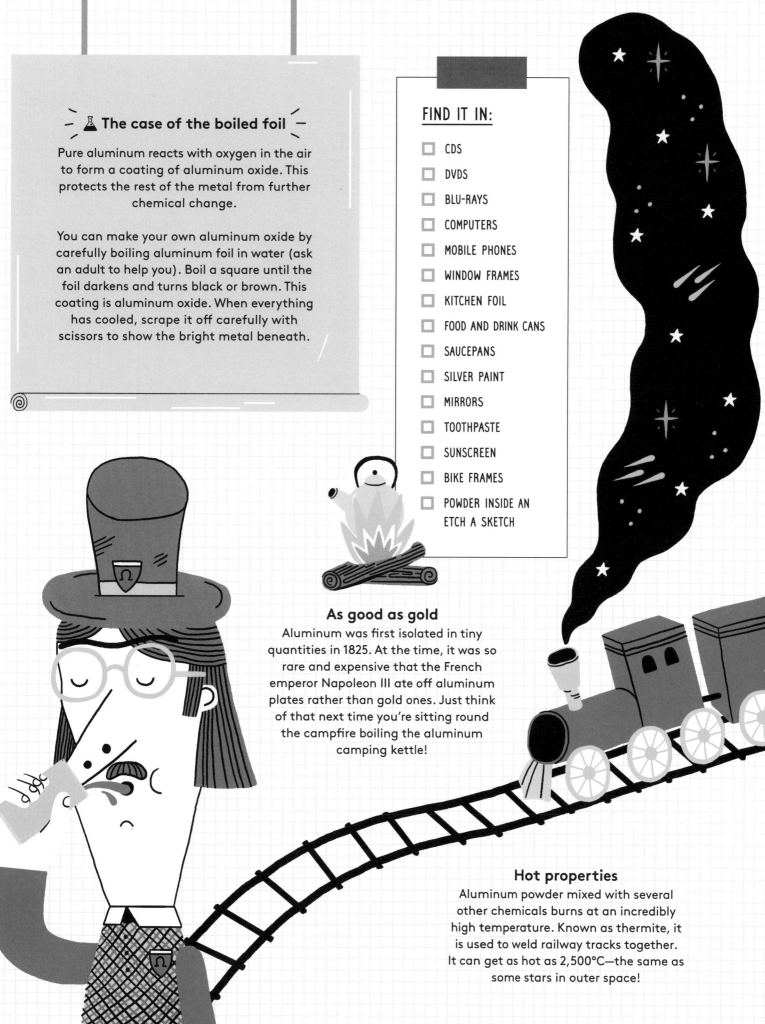

14 Si Silicon

👁 Blue-gray crystalline non-metal
⚠ Safe in most forms ☆ Computer genius

Silicon makes our modern world possible! As a "semiconductor" (meaning it can conduct electricity under certain circumstances), it is used in electronic equipment such as computers, mobile phones, and tablets. Miniature circuits are printed on tiny pieces of silicon, creating processors known as microchips.

Silicon also forms soft, rubber-like substances called silicones. These are used to make non-scratch, non-stick cooking utensils, flexible baking molds, soft contact lenses, charity wristbands, and even babies' bottles and pacifiers.

Sand is the main material used in the production of glass, which can be made naturally when lightning strikes a beach and melts the sand!

🔍 The case of the sandy beach

Take a trip to the beach and you'll find silicon gets everywhere! That's because silicon combines with oxygen to form silicon dioxide (SiO_2), better known as sand. Sand is made of tiny grains of silicon-containing minerals, with quartz and feldspar the most common.

FIND IT IN:

- ☐ CUCUMBERS
- ☐ SAND
- ☐ QUARTZ
- ☐ PRECIOUS STONES
- ☐ GLAZED POTTERY
- ☐ PLATES
- ☐ PORCELAIN
- ☐ MOBILE PHONES
- ☐ COMPUTERS
- ☐ TABLETS
- ☐ TVS
- ☐ CAT LITTER
- ☐ COOKWARE
- ☐ WRISTBANDS
- ☐ BABY EQUIPMENT
- ☐ NETTLES

Phosphorus 15 P

👁 Variously colored non-metal
⚠ Poisonous ☆ Underwater fire

As it was the thirteenth element isolated by early chemists, superstitious people called it "The Devil's Element." As if to prove them right, it has two main allotropes—white and red—both highly toxic and so reactive that they burn in air, and even underwater!

Phosphorus is essential to all living things, as it's part of DNA and helps to release energy from cells. Despite this, animals—including humans—excrete almost all the phosphorus they consume each day!

🔍 Strike a light

You can track down phosphorus in a box of safety matches. The match head contains phosphorus sesquisulfide (P_4S_3). The striking surface on the box has more phosphorus, plus glue and tiny glass particles. These produce heat from friction when the match is struck, lighting the tip.

FIND IT IN:

- ☐ YOU
- ☐ BONE CHINA
- ☐ PLANT FOOD
- ☐ SAFETY MATCHES
- ☐ DOGS
- ☐ CATS
- ☐ POOP
- ☐ PEE
- ☐ COLA

(WARNING! Do not drink it!)

⚗ The case of the coin in the cola

The ingredients of cola include a dilute solution of phosphoric acid (H_3PO_4), a compound that is also used to remove rust from metal. To prove its devilish power, leave some dirty coins in a glass of cola for a few days. Pour away the dirty cola, and see how sparkling the coins are.

Sulfur

◉ Yellow crystalline non-metal
⚠ Essential for life ☆ Super smells

One of the ancient elements known to alchemists, who first called it brimstone, sulfur is found in hot springs and volcanoes. Because of this, people used to think it bubbled up from some underground hell.

The yellow element itself does not smell, but many of its compounds do—including stinky substances in rotten eggs, garlic, cooked cabbage, bad breath, and farts. Despite this drawback, sulfur is part of essential substances such as many vitamins and proteins.

Flash in the pan

Sulfur is mixed with charcoal and saltpeter to make the gunpowder that adds the fizz to fireworks. That's why the air smells strongly of sulfur dioxide after a firework display. Safety matches also contain sulfur and smell bad when you blow them out. For this reason, some people light a match so that the stinky SO_2 masks a bad toilet smell!

FIND IT IN:

☐ HAIR
☐ FUR
☐ FEATHERS
☐ BAD BREATH
☐ FARTS
☐ EGGS
☐ CABBAGE
☐ ASPARAGUS
☐ SAFETY MATCHES

🧪 The case of the smelly feather

Many proteins in humans and animals are made from building bricks called "amino acids," which contain sulfur. Hair, fur, and feathers are all formed from proteins. With an adult present, hold the tip of a feather in a candle flame. As the sulfur compounds are released, you will smell the same horrible smell as when your hair gets too hot under a hairdryer.

Chlorine

◉ Greeny-yellow gas
⚠ Toxic and choking
☆ Bacteria destroying

Chlorine comes under fluorine in the Periodic Table and is nearly as nasty. It is very reactive and mostly found in compounds, including table salt. Chlorine gets its name from the Greek for "pale green," the color of the elemental gas, which is highly dangerous if inhaled and was used as a weapon in World War I.

The chlorine found in bleach is effective at killing many micro-organisms, even when very diluted. That's why it is often added to swimming pools—the drawback being that the chlorine bonds with the proteins in your skin and hair to leave you smelling of the pool.

Because it is so brilliant at biffing bacteria, chlorine is used to make drinking water safe and can be found in household cleaning products.

Particularly Versatile Chlorine

PVC (polyvinyl chloride) is a polymer formed from chlorine, carbon, and hydrogen atoms. The long chains of molecules produce a plastic with lots of applications, including drainpipes, flooring, furniture,, and many toys. Most "rubber" ducks are made from PVC!

FIND IT IN:

☐ TABLE SALT
☐ BLEACH
☐ CLEANING PRODUCTS
☐ TAP WATER
☐ DRAINPIPES
☐ VINYL FLOORING
☐ VINYL SOFAS
☐ PVC JACKETS
☐ RUBBER DUCKS

SIR ISAAC NEWTON (GRAVITY, APPLE) WAS THE GREATEST SCIENTIST OF HIS DAY, YET EVEN SIR ISAAC DABBLED IN ALCHEMY.

(THE SEVENTEENTH CENTURY)

FELLOW SCIENTIFIC BIGWIG ROBERT BOYLE (1627–1691) ALSO ATTEMPTED ALCHEMY BUT HE HAD HIS DOUBTS....

*BRITISH SPELLING OF "SKEPTICAL"
**OLD-STYLE SPELLING OF "CHEMIST"

UNLIKE THE ALCHEMISTS, BOYLE WASN'T THAT INTERESTED IN MAKING GOLD.

TRUE—HIS DAD WAS A RICH NOBLEMAN.

BOYLE EXPERIMENTED METHODICALLY, MADE NOTES AND SHARED HIS RESULTS WITH OTHER SCIENTISTS, MAKING HIM THE FIRST MODERN CHEMIST.

BOYLE THOUGHT THE KNOWN ELEMENTS EACH HAD PARTICLES OF DIFFERENT SHAPES AND SIZES...

JUST LIKE THE ANCIENT GREEKS!

BOYLE MADE PROGRESS, BUT ALCHEMISTS STILL CAME UP WITH CRAZY NEW IDEAS SUCH AS "PHLOGISTON" – A FIRE-LIKE "ELEMENT" SET FREE WHEN STUFF BURNED.

ACCORDING TO SOME, A CANDLE IN A CLOSED CONTAINER WENT OUT BECAUSE THE AIR AROUND IT COULDN'T ABSORB ANY MORE PHLOGISTON.

CHEMISTS AT THE TIME THOUGHT ALL GASES WERE DIFFERENT TYPES OF AIR. THE WORD "GAS" BECAME COMMON MUCH LATER.

IN THE 1770S ENGLISH CHEMIST JOSEPH PRIESTLEY ISOLATED A GAS THAT HE CALLED "DEPHLOGISTICATED AIR" AS IT ENCOURAGED COMBUSTION.

BUT A FRENCH CHEMIST* TOOK A DIM VIEW OF PHLOGISTON...

*ANTOINE-LAURENT DE LAVOISIER (1743–1794)

LAVOISIER IDENTIFIED PRIESTLEY'S AIR AS AN ELEMENT AND GAVE IT OUR MODERN NAME, "OXYGEN." HE ALSO RENAMED SO-CALLED "FLAMMABLE AIR," "HYDROGEN." JUST AS WELL WHEN IT COMES TO H_2O!

LAVOISIER DEBUNKED PHLOGISTON AND ALL THE ANCIENT GREEK NONSENSE AND INSTEAD NAMED 55 SUBSTANCES AS ACTUAL CHEMICAL ELEMENTS. CLEVER STUFF, BUT SADLY HE WAS GUILLOTINED IN THE FRENCH REVOLUTION.

Ar *18* Argon

◉ Colorless, odorless, tasteless gas
⚠ Bores you to death ☆ Super lazy

Like helium and neon, argon is an inert noble gas. It is totally unreactive with other substances and has a very suitable name: argon means "lazy."

Argon atoms are made in huge stellar explosions across the universe, but most argon in our atmosphere is made when radioactive potassium-40 decays in the Earth's crust. These radioactive isotopes have a "half-life" of over 1.3 billion years, so we won't be running out any time soon!

FIND IT IN:

☐ AIR
☐ LIGHT BULBS
☐ FOOD PACKAGING
☐ DOUBLE-GLAZED WINDOWS

What is a half-life?
Elementary! This is the time it takes for half the number of atoms in a radioactive isotope to decay. Radioactive material with a half-life of millions of years remains deadly dangerous for a long, long time, which is why the radioactive waste from nuclear power stations is such a problem. (See pages 58–59 for more clues.)

🔍 Secret code
Because argon is so unreactive, it replaces air in some packaging to keep foods fresher for longer. In Europe, you can look for its code (E938) to discover it in a can.

K *19* Potassium

◉ Soft silvery metal ⚠ Highly reactive, burns on water ☆ Super balance

Potassium reacts so rapidly with water and air that it exists only as compounds in nature. It is essential to us, as it helps our nerves send signals to our brains.

Potassium takes its name from "potash," as potassium salts were once made by boiling wood ash in a pot until all the water evaporated. And its symbol is K because scientists love using Latin. Potash in Latin is *kalium*.

K for ka-boom
Potassium nitrate (KNO_3), or saltpeter, is one of the three ingredients of gunpowder. You will find it in fireworks and plant fertilizer, and in preserved foods such as sausages and cured meats.

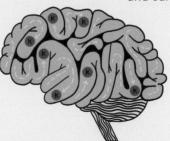

Why do tennis players eat bananas?
Elementary! Potassium ions (potassium atoms with electrons missing) help to keep our bodies' chemicals balanced and our blood pressure level. They can be lost when we sweat, so sports players eat and drink potassium-rich things to replace them. One of the best natural sources is bananas. Milk, potatoes, avocados, almonds, pistachios, and chocolate are also potassium-rich snacks.

FIND IT IN:

☐ YOU
☐ ANIMALS
☐ BLOOD
☐ SWEAT
☐ PEE
☐ POOP
☐ PLANTS
☐ PLANT FOOD
☐ BANANAS
☐ CHOCOLATE
☐ MILK
☐ POTATOES
☐ AVOCADOS
☐ FOOD ADDITIVES
☐ FIREWORKS

Calcium

20 Ca

👁 Soft silvery metal
⚠ Reactive ☆ Bone forming

Calcium is found in compounds in rocks and minerals such as marble, chalk, and limestone—the stuff we make buildings and bridges from.

Calcium phosphate is found in our teeth and bones, so growing children need plenty of it. Foods full of calcium include milk, yogurt, cheese, broccoli, kale, seaweed, and tinned sardines.

FIND IT IN:

- ☐ YOUR SKELETON AND TEETH
- ☐ EGGS
- ☐ DAIRY PRODUCTS
- ☐ LEAFY VEGETABLES
- ☐ WALLS
- ☐ TAP WATER
- ☐ LIMESCALE
- ☐ TOOTHPASTE
- ☐ COSMETICS
- ☐ PLASTER CASTS
- ☐ SCUMMY BATH RING

If you have a marble worktop in your kitchen, it mostly contains calcium carbonate ($CaCO_3$), the same substance that snails build their shells from.

🧪 The case of the vanishing shell

An eggshell is made almost entirely from calcium carbonate. Place clean pieces of shell in a glass filled with vinegar. Small bubbles of gas (carbon dioxide) should appear. A soluble compound will form, dissolving away the shell. Leave it in vinegar for a day or so and the shell should vanish.

🔍 Hard luck

"Hard water" contains lots of dissolved calcium. When the water is heated, the calcium may form a chalky substance called limescale. So if you want to track down calcium, look inside a cold kettle. Calcium in hard water will also react with a chemical in soap, producing calcium stearate. That's what leaves a ring round the bath!

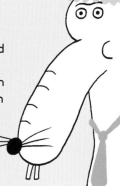

Scandium

21 Sc

👁 Soft silvery metal
⚠ Do not inhale ☆ Expensive alloy

Scandium takes its name from "Scandinavia," where the element was discovered in 1879, though its existence had been predicted ten years earlier by Dmitri Mendeleev, the creator of the Periodic Table.

It's very rare, which makes it very expensive. Some scandium is alloyed with aluminum to make fighter jets and sports equipment.

FIND IT IN:

- ☐ BASEBALL BATS
- ☐ GOLF CLUBS
- ☐ FISHING RODS

Titanium

22 Ti

◉ Hard silvery metal ⚠ Safe to implant
☆ Bionic body parts

Many of the minerals made by volcanoes contain titanium, and it's been found in some moon rocks too. The elemental metal makes some amazing alloys. Titanium oxide (TiO_2) is a bright-white compound that finds its way into many domestic products.

Hip op

Alloyed with aluminum, titanium is used to make artificial knee and hip joints. Titanium is also used in dental implants—false teeth that fuse over time with the jaw bone, leaving your body partly made of metal. If you're looking for clues, try asking your grandparents!

FIND IT IN:

- ☐ WHITE PAINT
- ☐ TOOTHPASTE
- ☐ LAPTOP CASES
- ☐ SPECTACLE FRAMES
- ☐ JEWELRY
- ☐ ARTIFICIAL HIPS, KNEES, TEETH

Vanadium

23 V

◉ Hard silvery-gray metal
⚠ Some toxic compounds ☆ Super tough

Elemental vanadium rarely occurs naturally, but vanadium compounds are important in industrial processes such as making sulfuric acid. Although it was named after a goddess of beauty, vanadium is alloyed with steel to make super-tough tools such as wrenches and spanners. Check the shed for clues!

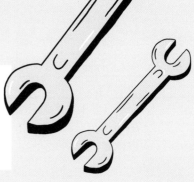

FIND IT IN:

- ☐ TOUGH TOOLS

Chromium

24 Cr

◉ Hard silvery-gray metal
⚠ Some toxic compounds ☆ Color caster

Some natural chromium can be found on Earth, but this element is mostly mined as minerals from which an amazing array of colorful compounds can be formed. Its name means "color," and chromium compounds range through the rainbow from red to violet. Tiny traces of chromium are responsible for the red of rubies and the green of emeralds.

FIND IT IN:

- ☐ SHINY, CHROMIUM-PLATED PARTS
- ☐ POTS, PANS, SINKS
- ☐ RUBIES

Alloy there!

Alloyed with steel, chromium makes stainless steel, which is not only strong but brilliantly rustproof. The metal was once widely applied on super-shiny car bumpers.

Manganese

25 Mn

◉ Silvery-gray metal
⚠ Too much is toxic
☆ Strong alloy

Manganese, like magnesium, takes its name from the place in ancient Greece where it was once mined.

Alloy there!

Most of the manganese made today goes into alloys. You will find it in certain stainless steels and in aluminum alloys used to make drinks cans. Adding manganese along with traces of other metals, such as copper and iron, allows the can wall to be made thinner while still being strong.

FIND IT IN:

- ☐ ALUMINUM DRINKS CANS
- ☐ ZINC-CARBON BATTERIES
- ☐ WALNUTS

BORN POOR IN ENGLAND IN 1766, FUTURE SUPER-CHEMIST JOHN DALTON WAS FORCED INTO WORK AS A CHILD. AGED JUST 12, HE BECAME A TEACHER!

Don't worry, Dalton, you'll soon grow into them...

HE DID! BY THE AGE OF 16 HE WAS RUNNING HIS OWN SCHOOL.

AS AN ADULT HE TAUGHT SCIENCE AND WAS OBSESSED WITH RECORDING THE WEATHER – WHICH HE DID EVERY DAY FOR THE REST OF HIS LIFE.

MON: RAIN
TUES: RAIN
WEDS: RAIN
THURS: ~~SUN~~ RAIN
INK

HE LIVED NEAR ENGLAND'S BEAUTIFUL – BUT SOGGY – LAKE DISTRICT.

BY STUDYING THE ATMOSPHERE, DALTON HIT ON A BIG IDEA.

The air is a mix of different gases each made up of tiny particles – plus a lot of rain... BRR!

THE GAS PARTICLES MOVE ABOUT AND EXERT A PRESSURE.

YOU CAN DEMONSTRATE DALTON'S THEORY BY SCRUNCHING A DRY TISSUE INTO THE BOTTOM OF AN UPENDED GLASS AND HOLDING IT UNDERWATER.

THE GAS PUSHES BACK! THE TISSUE STAYS DRY!

NEXT DALTON ARGUED THAT IF GASES HAD TINY PARTICLES, WHY NOT ALL MATTER?

Where did you get this amazing new idea?

The ancient Greeks.

TRUE! SEE ATOMIC COMIC #1!

IN 1803, DALTON CAME UP WITH AN UPDATED ATOMIC THEORY.

1. Elements have atoms. They're tiny!
2. An element's atoms are all alike.
3. Atoms can't be made or destroyed.
4. Atoms combine in set ways to make compounds.
5. Atoms are at the heart of chemical reactions.
6. chalk runs in the rain.
   ← CALCIUM SULFATE

MOST OF IT STILL HOLDS, ESPECIALLY THE LAST BIT!

DALTON ALSO SUGGESTED DIFFERENT ATOMIC WEIGHTS FOR ELEMENTS BY COMPARING THEM ALL TO HYDROGEN.

Hydrogen is number 1 with me!

AND HE GAVE ALL THE OTHER ELEMENTS LITTLE CIRCULAR SYMBOLS...

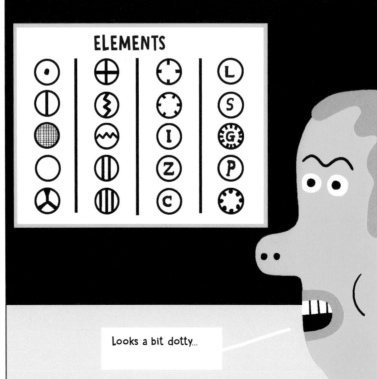

ELEMENTS

Looks a bit dotty...

LUCKILY A SWEDISH CHEMIST CALLED JACOB BERZELIUS HAD A BETTER IDEA...

16
S
32.065
Sulfur

"S" is "S"impler!

DALTON DID ALL THIS DESPITE BEING COLOR BLIND AND ONLY EVER SEEING THE WORLD IN THE COLORS OF THIS COMIC – YELLOW, BLUE, AND PURPLE!

Unlike the weather, it turned out fine.

DALTON DIED IN 1844, AND NOW HAS HIS OWN CRATER ON THE MOON!

Iron

26 **Fe**

◉ Silvery-gray metal
⚠ Safe ☆ Magnetic attraction

Iron is the finale of the fusion process that occurs within stars. After creating iron, they collapse and explode, spraying the element across space. Iron is the most abundant metal in the universe. Earth's inner and outer cores are largely a giant molten globe of iron and nickel, and there's plenty of iron in the crust too.

Over 4 billion years since the Earth first formed, space is still sending us iron. About one in every twenty meteorites that lands on the planet is a big lump of iron and nickel. In the ancient world, people prized iron as a gift from the gods.

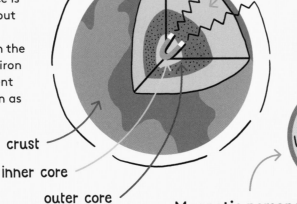

mantle

crust

inner core

outer core

Why do we turn iron into steel?

Elementary! Steel is stronger than iron and often more resistant to rust. Adding carbon and other elements in small quantities to iron creates different types of steel. Stainless steel, with small amounts of chromium and manganese, doesn't rust at all. That's why we use it to construct buildings, bridges, cars, cutlery, and pans.

Blood and iron

Iron is essential to hemoglobin, the molecule in red blood cells that carries oxygen around our bodies. It's also why our blood and many meats we eat are red. Foods high in iron include meat, fish, leafy vegetables such as spinach, and dark chocolate.

Rusty reactions

What we call rust chemists call hydrated iron oxide (Fe_2O_3). The presence of water molecules means that strong silvery-looking iron reacts chemically to give weak, flaky red rust. That is why iron is protected from air and moisture by painting, galvanizing (*see page 36*) or adding other elements to create alloys.

Magnetic personality

Iron and many of its compounds and alloys such as steel are magnetic. Magnetism is a peculiar property of some substances caused by the way electrons are aligned inside atoms. The iron core of the Earth acts as a giant magnet, producing an invisible magnetic field that can be detected with a compass.

FIND IT IN:

☐ YOU
☐ BLOOD
☐ MEATS
☐ LEAFY VEGETABLES
☐ DARK CHOCOLATE
☐ BREAKFAST CEREALS
☐ RUST
☐ FRIDGES
☐ CUTLERY
☐ POTS AND PANS
☐ PAPER CLIPS

🧪 **The case of the rusty wool**

See for yourself how quickly iron can rust. Ask an adult to help you carefully pour boiling water over a small ball of steel wool in a bowl. (Steel wool is made of matted iron fibers with a low carbon content and is used for cleaning.) Let the wool stand in the water while it cools. After a few hours, orangey-red rust particles will start to form.

Cobalt

27 Co

👁 Hard silvery-gray metal
⚠ Necessary ☆ Vital vitamin

Cobalt gets its name from "Kobold," the German word for "goblin," as some of the compounds in which it is found were present in mines where these mythical mischievous midgets were said to live.

FIND IT IN:

- ☐ MEAT, FISH, DAIRY
- ☐ LITHIUM-ION BATTERIES
- ☐ BLUE POTS AND GLASSWARE
- ☐ COBALT-BLUE PAINT

Cobalt is a key part of the vitamin ("*vital-mineral*") B12, which can't be manufactured by our bodies, only by certain micro-organisms. We get most of our B12 from eating meat, fish, and dairy products, though it can also be made synthetically. Vegans (people who don't eat animal products) are often advised to take B12 supplements.

Feeling blue

Rocks and minerals containing cobalt have been used for thousands of years to add fantastic blue colors to crafts. Cobalt gives a deep-blue hue to glass and forms a gorgeous glaze on pottery. There is also a color of paint called "cobalt blue," containing cobalt aluminate ($CoAl_2O_4$), which was a favorite of the Dutch painter Vincent van Gogh.

Nickel

28 Ni

👁 Hard silvery-golden metal
⚠ Can cause rashes ☆ Super magnetic

Nickel seems fickle. There's hardly any in the Earth's crust, and yet our planet's core is a giant molten mix of nickel and iron. Like iron, nickel is magnetic and it is often alloyed with iron and other metals to make very strong magnets.

Guilty as charged!

Nickel compounds are also used in rechargeable batteries. Nickel was often combined with cadmium to produce NiCd batteries, but the poisonous cadmium could leak from discarded batteries. Nickel–metal hydride batteries (NiMH) are an improvement, but all used batteries should always be taken to a proper recycling point for disposal.

Nickel appears to be essential for plants, and possibly for animals, but only in tiny amounts. Large doses can be toxic, and while nickel is used in earrings, occasionally people with pierced ears will suffer an allergic reaction to it.

🔍 Coining it in

The coin called a nickel (worth 5 cents) contains only 25% nickel, the rest being copper, but the coins are still silvery in color. British silver coins used to contain copper, but more recent silver coins have a steel center with a nickel coating. So you can hunt for this element in your coins by using a magnet.

FIND IT IN:

- ☐ COINS
- ☐ NiMH BATTERIES
- ☐ ALNICO MAGNETS
- ☐ JEWELRY

Copper

^{29}Cu

◉ Reddish soft metal
⚠ Safe ☆ Super conductor

Humans have known about copper for over 10,000 years. Bronze—an alloy of copper and tin—gave its name to an Age of history, and copper is even more important to civilization today. It carries the current in our high-tech devices, it cables the internet across the globe, and it pipes the running water to our sinks.

FIND IT IN:

- ☐ LIVER
- ☐ LOBSTERS
- ☐ OYSTERS
- ☐ KALE
- ☐ RAISINS
- ☐ PRUNES
- ☐ PLUMBING
- ☐ BRONZE
- ☐ BRASS
- ☐ TRUMPET
- ☐ TROMBONE
- ☐ CYMBALS
- ☐ BELLS
- ☐ ANYTHING ELECTRICAL
- ☐ ANYTHING ELECTRONIC
- ☐ SAUCEPANS
- ☐ COINS
- ☐ ZIPS
- ☐ STATUE OF LIBERTY

Musical clues

If you want to search for copper clues, use your ears. Bronze, an alloy of copper mixed with tin, is used in musical instruments, especially bells and cymbals. Brass, an alloy of copper and zinc, has its own section in the orchestra, which includes the trumpet, trombone, and tuba. And as brass is good at resisting the weather, you will also hear it used as a door knocker!

🧪 The case of the cool candle

Chemists test some substances by putting them in flames. Compounds with copper in them produce a blue-green color and are often added to fireworks.

However, if you strip the coating off a 6 inch length of pure copper wire, coil it into a small cone and hold it over a lit candle, it can reduce the flame (ask an adult to help you). The copper conducts heat away from the flame, cooling it down. Remove the coil and it should come back to life.

WARNING! Get an adult to help, and don't touch the flame.

Blue-blooded

For snails, crabs, and lobsters, copper plays the same role in their blood as iron does in ours. Only their blood is blue! Foods rich in copper include liver, lobsters (obviously), oysters, kale, avocados, raisins, plums, and prunes.

Given the verdigris

Copper and gold are the only metal elements not silvery in color. When exposed to oxygen in the air, copper forms a green compound called "verdigris." Some old buildings have copper roofs that have now turned green. That's also why the Statue of Liberty now looks a bit seasick. She was originally a dull coppery brown.

Zinc

👁 Soft bluish-gray metal
⚠ Essential ☆ Super protector

There are many zinc-containing minerals and mining them is an important and very old business. Ancient people alloyed zinc with copper to make brass, which we still use today.

Zinc assists in many important processes in cells. Plants grow poorly in soils without zinc. It assists our brain function and reproduction, and in making DNA, the blueprint for our bodies. Some people believe it also helps fight off colds.

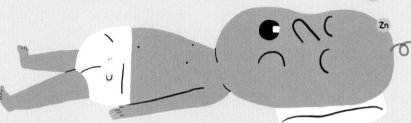

FIND IT IN:

- ☐ MEAT
- ☐ FISH
- ☐ OYSTERS
- ☐ WHEAT
- ☐ SPINACH
- ☐ SUNFLOWER SEEDS
- ☐ PEANUTS
- ☐ PARMESAN CHEESE
- ☐ GALVANIZED ITEMS
- ☐ ANYTHING BRASS
- ☐ SUNBLOCK
- ☐ DIAPER RASH CREAMS
- ☐ ANTI-DANDRUFF SHAMPOOS

Zinc or skin

Zinc oxide (ZnO) is a common zinc compound that is very useful for our skin. It is used in sunscreens and sunblock, reflecting ultraviolet light and stopping skin from burning. It also soothes some of the most sensitive skin around babies' bottoms, as it is the main ingredient in creams for diaper rash.

WARNING! Never touch your tongue to any electrical terminals or other devices.

🧪 The case of the electric lemon

Build your own battery using 3 galvanized (zinc-plated) nails, 3 lengths of copper wire, and 3 lemons. Push a nail into each lemon, joining it to the next lemon with the copper wire. Push the free end of the wire into the lemon near to but not touching the nail. Each zinc/copper/lemon unit forms an electrical cell. Joined in a series like this, they form a battery.

The zinc and iron react with the acids in the lemon to produce a small electric current that will flow if you touch your tongue across the zinc and copper end terminals. You should just feel a little tingle.

Getting galvanized

Half the world's zinc is used to protect iron or steel from rusting by "galvanizing"—coating them in a thin layer of zinc. Zinc is more chemically reactive with water and air than iron, producing a compound that acts as a protective barrier against rain.

You can track down galvanized clues in lamp posts, ladders, nails, waste bins, wheelbarrows, and corrugated roofing. Look for their dull-gray surfaces!

A CLEVER CORNISH CHEMIST PUT A LOT OF ENERGY INTO ISOLATING NEW ELEMENTS...

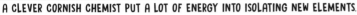

SIR HUMPHRY DAVY, BORN CORNWALL, ENGLAND, 1778

DAVY USED ELECTRICAL ENERGY GENERATED BY THE NEW SCIENTIFIC TOOL, THE VOLTAIC PILE*...

*NAMED AFTER ITALIAN INVENTOR ALESSANDRO VOLTA, 1745–1827

THE PILE WAS A SIMPLE BATTERY MADE FROM ALTERNATE DISCS OF TWO METALS, ZINC, AND COPPER, WITH WET FABRIC BETWEEN.

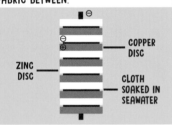

IT WORKED LIKE THE LEMON BATTERY (SEE PAGE 36).

IN 1807, DAVY USED POTS OF PILES TO PASS A STRONG CURRENT THROUGH SUPER-HOT MOLTEN CAUSTIC POTASH (SEE PAGE 29)... NO GOGGLES, NO SCREENS, NOTHING...

CHEMISTS CALL THIS PROCESS ~~CRAZY~~ "ELECTROLYSIS."

TINY GRAY GLOBULES FORMED. DAVY HAD ISOLATED THE FIRST SAMPLES OF A HIGHLY REACTIVE METAL...

BUT COULD HE DO IT AGAIN?

DAYS LATER, DAVY ELECTROLYZED MOLTEN CAUSTIC SODA, AND THIS TIME...

MORE FOLLOWED...

SOON AFTER...

AND ON HE WENT...

IN 1808...

THEN...

NEXT TIME...

MORE?

YES! AGAIN IN 1808...

BUT THAT NOW WAS FINALLY IT...

ER, UNTIL A FEW YEARS LATER, WHEN...

DAVY WAS AN INCREDIBLE CHEMIST AND WAS KNIGHTED FOR HIS MANY DISCOVERIES.

BUT THERE WAS ONE ELEMENT HE DIDN'T DISCOVER, BUT MAYBE SHOULD HAVE....

*THE CHEMICAL SYMBOL FOR ARGON. DAVY DIED IN 1829. ARGON WAS DISCOVERED IN 1894.

(PS: IN REAL LIFE, DAVY MAY OR MAY NOT HAVE HAD A STRONG CORNISH ACCENT.)

Gallium

³¹ Ga

👁 Soft silvery-blue metal
⚠ Non-toxic ☆ Laser power

In 1871, Dmitri Mendeleev predicted the existence of both gallium and germanium before they had been discovered. French chemist Paul-Emile Lecoq de Boisbaudran isolated gallium four years later, naming it for France (aka Gaul).

Gallium is a solid at room temperature, but only just: at 86°F it melts. The human body has a temperature of 98.6°F, so this is incredibly useful: gallium metal (which isn't poisonous) can be used to replace liquid mercury (which is) in thermometers.

Gallium gadgets

You can track down gallium nitride (GaN) in LED lights and lasers. The light it produces is violet rather than blue, but the gallium lasers used to read Blu-ray discs give them their name. The lasers read tiny holes on the surface of the discs.

FIND IT IN:

☐ SAFE THERMOMETERS

☐ MICROCHIPS

☐ BLU-RAY DISC PLAYERS

Germanium

³² Ge

👁 Shiny silvery metalloid
⚠ Safe at low levels ☆ Superfast

Germanium and gallium have a lot in common. Both were predicted by Dmitri Mendeleev, and both were named after the country of the chemist who first isolated them. (German chemist Clemens Winkler discovered germanium in 1886.) Both elements are used in transistors and microchips—the first working transistor was made in 1947 with a crystal of germanium.

Watch it!

Germanium is a component in the fiber-optic cables used for the internet and on-demand TV. These have a central core containing silica, to which the compound germanium oxide is added. So if you have superfast broadband, you can detect germanium by watching TV!

FIND IT IN:

☐ TRANSISTORS

☐ HIGH-TECH EQUIPMENT

☐ FIBER-OPTIC CABLES

Arsenic

³³ As

👁 Gray, yellow or black metalloid
⚠ Deadly ☆ Potent poison

Arsenic is an ancient element that has been poisoning people for thousands of years! Many of its compounds can be deadly, too. Some occur in the Earth's crust, and in some regions millions of people are affected by water contaminated by minerals containing arsenic. There is also arsenic in the sea and air, often due to smoke from volcanoes.

Deadly arsenic

Arsenic is just one of the many toxins in cigarette smoke, as tobacco plants take up arsenic from the soil. Arsenic compounds were once prescribed in medicines and used to kill everything from microbes to mice before they were largely banned worldwide. They were also a favorite poison in murder plots! You might track down the name on an old chemist's jar.

> It was used in rat poison too!

FIND IT IN:

☐ SMOKE

☐ POISONS

☐ MICROCHIPS

Selenium

³⁴ Se

👁 Silvery metalloid
⚠ Too much is toxic
☆ Completely nuts

Selenium is a rare element in the Earth's crust, almost as uncommon as gold. Too much can be toxic, but some scientists think we need traces to stay healthy. Foods high in selenium include tuna, sardines, eggs, spinach, and Brazil nuts.

FIND IT IN

☐ BRAZIL NUTS

☐ TUNA

☐ SARDINES

☐ SPINACH

☐ CHICKEN

☐ GRASS-FED BEE

☐ EGGS

☐ ANTI-DANDRUF SHAMPOOS (SO CONTAIN SELENIUM DISU (SES₂) WHICH KNOCKS Oʊ CERTAIN FUNGI)...

⚗ The case of the burning Brazil nut

Brazil nuts aren't just high in selenium but also in natural oils—so much so that they can be used as a torch. Lay one on a plate and hold a burning match to one end (ask an adult to help). The oil in the nut will catch fire and give a strong light. It will burn for a very long time, so make sure you blow it out afterwards and don't touch the hot nut.

Bromine

35 Br

👁 Smelly brown liquid
⚠ Toxic, burns ☆ Super smelly

Bromine is one of only two elements that are liquid at room temperature (77°F). It is found in seawater, though in smaller quantities than its related element chlorine. Bromine is sometimes added to the water in pools and hot-tubs to keep down the growth of nasty bacteria.

FIND IT IN:

- ☐ HOT-TUBS AND POOLS
- ☐ TVS
- ☐ COMPUTERS
- ☐ FLAME RETARDANTS

Krypton

36 Kr

👁 Colorless, odorless gas
⚠ Non-toxic ☆ Energy efficient

Is it a bird? Is it a plane? No, it's a noble gas. You might know Krypton as Superman's home planet, but unlike the fictional kryptonite—which sapped Superman's superpowers—real krypton isn't so alarming...

FIND IT IN:

- ☐ FLUORESCENT BULBS
- ☐ COMIC STRIPS

Rubidium

37 Rb

👁 Silvery-white metal
⚠ Uncertain ☆ Super scientific

Rubidium is in the same gang as sodium and potassium, and is just as reactive. Rubidium compounds mostly turn up as impurities in other minerals, making them harder to extract. But there isn't that much call for rubidium anyway. Rubidium nitrate ($RbNO_3$) turns fireworks purple, but otherwise most uses are super-scientific ones.

FIND IT IN:

- ☐ PURPLE FIREWORKS

Strontium

38 Sr

👁 Soft silvery-yellow metal
⚠ Radioactive ☆ Tooth repairer

Strontium is in the same group as calcium, and humans can store it in their bones in the same way. Because the body replaces calcium with strontium, strontium compounds are found in toothpastes for people with sensitive teeth, repairing them where enamel has worn away. Strontium compounds also give deep-red colors to fireworks.

FIND IT IN:

- ☐ SENSITIVE TOOTHPASTES
- ☐ RED FIREWORKS

Yttrium

39 Y

👁 Soft silvery metal
⚠ Can be toxic ☆ Picture painter

Yttrium is loved by Scrabble players! It takes its name from Ytterby, a village in Sweden where ores containing seven undiscovered elements were found. You might detect yttrium in an old-fashioned "cathode ray" TV, where it was part of the red phosphors that dotted the screen.

FIND IT IN:

- ☐ OLD TVS

Zirconium

40 Zr

👁 Hard silvery-gray metal
⚠ Radioactive isotopes ☆ Sweat fighter

Zirconium and some of its compounds are used in the linings of nuclear reactors. At home, you can find zirconium compounds in deodorants and antiperspirants, while zirconium dioxide (ZrO_2) is a beautiful colorless crystal that can be cut to look like a diamond.

FIND IT IN:

- ☐ DEODORANT
- ☐ "CUBIC ZIRCONIA" JEWELRY

Niobium

◉ Shiny gray metal ⚠ Some toxic compounds ☆ Space traveler

Niobium is used in making super-hard alloys that go into pipelines and spacecraft. Pure niobium is hypoallergenic, meaning it doesn't trigger the skin rashes that nickel causes in some people. So although it is expensive, you can discover niobium in nose rings and earrings.

FIND IT IN:

- ☐ BODY PIERCINGS
- ☐ EARRINGS
- ☐ NOSE RINGS
- ☐ SPACECRAFT

Molybdenum

⁴² Mo

◉ Shiny silvery metal ⚠ Essential element ☆ Plant assistant

Molybdenum in the soil helps plants such as peas, beans, and clover convert nitrogen in the air into molecules vital to living organisms. Humans need tiny amounts to make enzymes, and we can acquire it from various vegetables. You can also find molybdenum in super-strong steel alloys.

FIND IT IN:

- ☐ PEAS
- ☐ BEANS
- ☐ LENTIL
- ☐ VEGET
- ☐ BIKES
- ☐ CAR PA

Technetium

⁴³ Tc

◉ Silvery metal ⚠ Radioactive ☆ Super scanner

Technetium is extracted from spent uranium fuel rods in nuclear reactors. All its isotopes are radioactive and one of them, technetium-99m, is incredibly useful. It emits detectable gamma rays, so doctors can insert it into patients and use it to create scans of the inside of their bodies. The isotope has a very short half-life of only 6 hours, which means that after 6 hours only half of it is left—it vanishes quickly from the body.

FIND IT IN:

- ☐ MEDICAL TESTS

Ruthenium

⁴⁴ Ru

◉ Silvery metal ⚠ Toxic compounds ☆ Super writer

Ruthenium is a rock-hard, unreactive metal. It is added to alloys to make them more durable and turns up in special electrical components. Some expensive fountain pens have a tiny blob of ruthenium on the tip of their nibs, which resists wear and keeps the pen writing smoothly.

FIND IT IN:

- ☐ FOUNTAIN PEN NIBS

Rhodium

⁴⁵ Rh

◉ Silvery-white metal ⚠ Inert ☆ Super converter

Because it doesn't tarnish, some rhodium is used to coat jewelry, but most goes into catalytic converters in cars. These convert polluting exhaust fumes into less harmful gases that can be released into the air. Platinum and palladium are also used in catalytic converters, and all three metals are so expensive that they are recycled from cars that are scrapped.

FIND IT IN:

- ☐ JEWELRY
- ☐ CATALYTIC CONVERTERS

Palladium

⁴⁶ Pd

◉ Silvery-white metal ⚠ No known harm ☆ Super teeth

Most palladium is made as a by-product of processing other metal ores. It is used in catalytic converters, and in jewelry and expensive pen nibs, often as a coating for gold. You might detect it in your own mouth: dentists include a small percentage in metal amalgam fillings.

FIND IT IN:

- ☐ JEWELRY
- ☐ CATALYTIC CONVERTER
- ☐ PENS
- ☐ DENTAL FILLINGS

ATOMIC COMICS
THE BEARDED DETECTIVES:
THE CASE OF THE PERIODIC TABLE

IN DEVELOPING THE PERIODIC TABLE, IT HELPED TO HAVE A BEARD. THE BIGGER THE BETTER.

Well, that's hardly fair on us, is it?

SORRY...

FRENCH CHEMIST ALEXANDRE-EMILE BEGUYER DE CHANCOURTOIS (1820–1886) HAD A BIG NAME BUT ONLY A SMALL BEARD.

'Andsome, non?

BECAUSE OF THIS HE DIDN'T QUITE SUCCEED.

IN 1862, HE WAS THE FIRST PERSON TO PRODUCE A CHART OF THE KNOWN ELEMENTS ARRANGED IN ORDER OF THEIR ATOMIC WEIGHTS.

I call it my "Vis Tellurique."

I call it baffling, monsieur.

SADLY, HIS WORK WAS OVERLOOKED.

THE NEXT BEARDY TO HAVE A BASH WAS BRITISH CHEMIST JOHN NEWLANDS, WHO HAD A MUCH BIGGER BEARD. AND DID MUCH BETTER.

I have come up with a "Law of Octaves"!

PUBLISHED IN 1864, THIS GROUPED TOGETHER ELEMENTS WITH ATOMIC MASSES EIGHT PLACES APART.

HOWEVER, THERE WERE A NUMBER OF PROBLEMS...

You have put iron in the same group as oxygen – and your beard is not quite big enough! Tch!

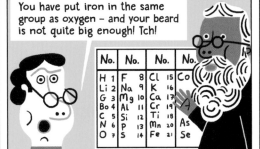

IT WAS A CLOSE SHAVE, BUT NEWLANDS HADN'T QUITE HIT ON IT.

LUCKILY HOTSHOT RUSSIAN CHEMIST DMITRI MENDELEEV* HAD A REALLY BIG BEARD, BIG HAIR, AND A BRAIN TO MATCH.

I need all this hair to keep it warm.

*PRONOUNCED DE-ME-TREE MEN-DEL-LAY-YEV (1834–1907)

IN 1867 MENDELEEV BEGAN WORK ON A NEW CHEMISTRY TEXTBOOK WHICH INVOLVED MAKING A FACT CARD FOR EVERY KNOWN ELEMENT...

I am sure there is a pattern to them – and I shall not sleep until I find it!

WHICH, OF COURSE, MEANT ONLY ONE THING...

ZZZZ...

ASLEEP, DMITRI DREAMED HE SAW THE CARDS REARRANGE THEMSELVES INTO A TABLE – WITH GAPS WHERE NEW ELEMENTS WERE STILL TO BE FOUND.

WELL, THAT'S THE STORY HE LIKED TO TELL!

IN 1869, DMITRI WENT PUBLIC WITH HIS PERIODIC TABLE, USING IT TO PREDICT THE EXISTENCE OF TWO UNKNOWN ELEMENTS TO FILL SOME OF HIS GAPS.

I have named them eka-aluminum and eka-silicon.

"EKA" MEANS "ONE AFTER" IN THE ANCIENT LANGUAGE OF SANSKRIT (DON'T ASK...)

NOT EVERYONE ACCEPTED MENDELEEV'S IDEAS UNTIL...

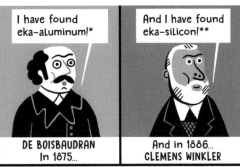

I have found eka-aluminum!*

And I have found eka-silicon!**

DE BOISBAUDRAN In 1875...

And in 1886... CLEMENS WINKLER

NOW KNOWN AS *GALLIUM, AND **GERMANIUM (SEE PAGE 38).

MENDELEEV'S TABLE HAD BEEN VALIDATED, AND TODAY HE HAS AN ELEMENT NAMED IN HIS HONOR.

ERBIUM	THULIUM	YTTERBIUM
100 Fm FERMIUM	101 Md "BIG BEARD IUM" MENDELEVIUM	102 No NOBELIUM

CAN YOU FIND IT IN YOUR TABLE?

⁴⁷Ag Silver

◉ Shiny silvery metal
⚠ Some toxic compounds
☆ Photographic memory

Use of silver dates back over 5,000 years. Its name comes from the Anglo-Saxon word "seolfor," while its symbol Ag comes from its Latin name "argentum," meaning silver or white. Because of its color alchemists associated it with the moon and gave it the sign of a crescent moon.

Silver is the most reflective of all the metals and is used to make mirrors. Silver reacts with sulfur compounds in the air, producing dark silver sulfide, so if you find an old mirror with a dark coating you may have discovered the element in the room.

> You can even eat silver. In Europe, it's food additive E174.

FIND IT IN:

- ☐ JEWELRY
- ☐ CUTLERY
- ☐ OLD PHOTOGRAPHS
- ☐ OLD COINS
- ☐ OLD MIRRORS
- ☐ BAND-AIDS
- ☐ CAKE DECORATIONS
- ☐ ODOR-ELIMINATING SOCKS

🔍 Old salts

Silver bromide (AgBr), silver chloride (AgCl), and silver iodide (AgI) are compounds present in photographic film and printing paper from the days before digital photography. The silver salts darken when they are exposed to light, either inside a camera (the film) or in a darkroom (the paper). Find an old black-and-white photograph and if you can see dark areas then you have detected crystals of silver salts.

⚗ The case of the tarnished spoon

Ask if you can borrow a silver or silver-plated spoon. Cut up and boil some sulfur-rich vegetables like cabbage or onions in a stainless steel pan of water. Remove from the heat and place your silver spoon in the smelly water.

Leave it immersed for a few hours, and a coating of silver sulfide will form where it is in contact with the sulfur-rich water, turning the spoon from dazzling to dark. Don't worry, you can restore it in the next experiment...

WARNING
Get an ad[u]
to help—t[h]
water wi[ll]
be hot.

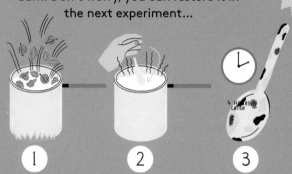

⚗ The case of the untarnished spoon

Line a mug with a sheet of aluminum foil. Fill another cup with warm water and stir in a spoonful of baking soda and a spoonful of salt. Pour this into the foil-lined cup. Dip the tarnished spoon into the solution so that it touches the foil. Small bubbles will appear on its surface, and the dark tarnish will fade before your eyes. A form of electrolysis is taking place. The silver sulfide is converted back to shiny silver, and the bubbles are hydrogen sulfide gas (the same gas given off by rotten eggs, as you can smell!).

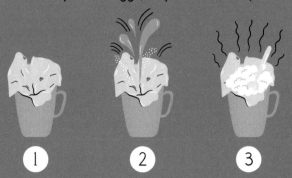

Cadmium

48 Cd

👁 Bluish-gray metal ⚠ Highly toxic ☆ Rechargeable

Cadmium is rare in the Earth's crust—and long may it stay that way. It is highly toxic and linked to many diseases, and its use is closely controlled. The biggest risk of general exposure comes from smoking. Cadmium is used to make rechargeable nickel-cadmium batteries (NiCd), which are safe in use but dangerous if not disposed of properly. Added to landfill they can pollute groundwater and poison crops and livestock.

Some brightly colored cadmium compounds are added to paints and plastics. Popular artists' pigments include cadmium yellow, cadmium orange, and cadmium red. They are safe to use as paints, but their use to color plastics, toys, and foodware has been restricted.

CADMIUM YELLOW

Indium

49 In

👁 Soft silvery-gray metal
⚠ Some toxic compounds ☆ Magic touch

Indium turns up in the Earth's crust in just a handful of minerals. Given its usefulness, some chemists worry supplies might run out within a century. Others say we'll just get better at extracting it. Weirdly, when you bend indium, the crystals moving inside the metal make a crackling sound. This makes it one of the few elements you can do an impression of!

Indium is soft like gallium. You can use it to write on paper and scratch it with a fingernail. It also sticks to the surface of glass, meaning you can make mirrors or reflective windows. But most indium is used to make indium tin oxide (ITO), a component in flat-screen TVs and the touchscreens of tablets and phones.

Tin

50 Sn

👁 Silvery-gray metal ⚠ Non-toxic ☆ Super fixer

Tin is an ancient element once prized for its use as an alloy with copper to produce bronze. Alloyed with copper and other metals, tin forms pewter, a soft, gray metal used to make plates, tankards, medallions, and model soldiers. Once hugely popular, it fell out of favor as it often contained toxic lead (not any more!).

A thin coating of tin can be used to protect iron and steel from rusting, and you will find it serving this purpose in tin cans (which were invented in the early nineteenth century and took their name from this element). Tin isn't magnetic but the steel in cans is, which is why you can pick them up with a magnet.

Solder, solder

Tin is found in almost every electrical or electronic device that has soldered contacts. Solder is an alloy of tin and lead that melts and sets rapidly to fix wires and microchips in place, and conducts electricity. As lead is potentially toxic, lead-free solder is widely used today.

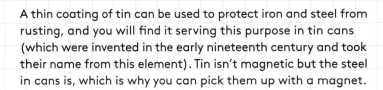

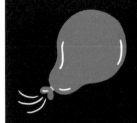
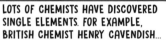

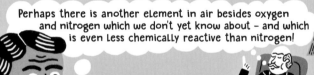
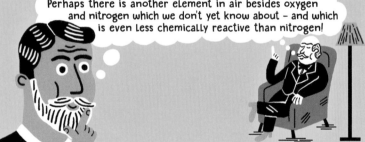

Antimony

51 Sb

👁 Silvery-gray metalloid
⚠ Potentially toxic
☆ Fireproof

Antimony is found in an ore called stibnite, which the ancient Egyptians turned into the black eye make-up (kohl) you see in figures on the walls of pyramids.

Stibnite is also the source of antimony's code name, Sb. You might detect it in the compound antimony trioxide (Sb_2O_3), which is applied to toys, clothing, and car seats to fireproof them.

FIND IT IN:

☐ TOYS, CLOTHING
☐ CAR SEATS
☐ CAR BATTERIES

Tellurium

52 Te

👁 Silvery-white metalloid
⚠ Toxic ☆ Super smelly

Tellurium is almost as rare on Earth as gold and platinum. It is one of the few elements that reacts with gold and forms ores from which gold can be extracted. Some tellurium goes into making alloys of steel, copper, and lead.

If you are exposed to too much tellurium in the air, your body will produce a chemical called dimethyl telluride, which makes your breath and sweat reek of garlic for months. Yuk!

FIND IT IN:

☐ REWRITABLE DVDS
☐ BLU-RAY DISCS

Iodine

53 I

👁 Black solid non-metal, violet gas
⚠ Essential for health ☆ Germ killer

Iodine is found in seawater and in the past was extracted from seaweed. Like fellow "halogens" chlorine and bromine it has a strong smell. Solutions of iodine are used to kill germs and can be applied directly to the skin, leaving a yellowy-brown stain. We need iodine so that our thyroid gland can produce the hormones that regulate growth and development. That's one reason iodine is often added to table salt.

Violet vapor

Elemental iodine does a strange thing. At room temperature, it is a purple-black solid. Heat it up and it turns directly into a violet vapor without first becoming a liquid—a process known as "sublimation."

FIND IT IN:

☐ YOU
☐ TABLE SALT
☐ COD
☐ HADDOCK
☐ EGGS
☐ YOGURT
☐ COW'S MILK
☐ FIRST-AID KIT

Xenon

54 Xe

👁 Colorless, inert gas
⚠ Non-toxic ☆ Super dazzling

Xenon is the only element beginning with X, but as an unreactive noble gas it isn't very X-citing. It is found in Earth's atmosphere in tiny traces, from where William Ramsay first X-tracted it in 1898 (see opposite), naming it after the Greek word for "stranger."

It is used in lasers, IMAX movie projectors, and spacecraft. Xenon headlamps on cars produce a dazzling light thanks to a dash of xenon in their bulbs. So perhaps it has a bright future!

FIND IT IN:

☐ AIR
☐ XENON HEADLAMPS
☐ IMAX MOVIE PROJECTORS

Xe Xe

Cesium

◉ Soft silvery-gold metal
⚠ Mildly toxic ☆ Time lord

55 Cs

Cesium is very reactive: add it to water and it explodes. You're unlikely to track down cesium atoms at home, but they do have a huge impact on you. Tiny changes in the energy of their electrons regulate so-called atomic clocks and keep them accurate to one second in tens of millions of years. These clocks coordinate mobile phone networks and the internet, so cesium controls your life!

FIND IT IN:

☐ INTERNET
☐ PHONE NETWORKS
☐ TIME

Barium

56 Ba

◉ Soft silvery metal ⚠ Toxic compounds
☆ X-ray specs

Barium takes its name from a Greek word meaning "heavy." Soluble barium compounds are poisonous, but insoluble barium sulfate is given to people having their insides X-rayed, as it lets doctors follow the path of food through the gut (a barium "meal"). Barium is alloyed with nickel in the spark plugs in cars and adds a lovely apple-green color to fireworks.

Check on barium's atomic number, and you'll see hafnium is 16 steps further on. The reason for this leap is the lanthanides, a group of elements with similar chemical properties resulting from the way they arrange their electrons. Chemists run them in a row under the main Periodic Table. (See page 54.)

FIND IT IN:

☐ SPARK PLUG
☐ FIREWORKS
☐ RAT POISON
☐ BARIUM MEAL

Hafnium

72 Hf

◉ Soft silvery metal
⚠ Not known to be toxic ☆ Space traveler

You'll struggle to find hafnium at home, so try using binoculars to look up at the surface of the moon. The thruster rockets of the Apollo lunar modules spacecraft had nozzles made of niobium, hafnium, and titanium. After safely transporting their crews back to the orbiter, some of these spacecraft were intentionally crashed on the moon. There's all sorts of stuff up there!

FIND IT IN:

☐ LUNAR SPACECRAFT

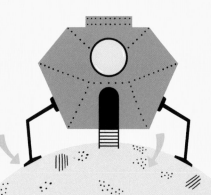

Tantalum

73 Ta

◉ Shiny gray metal
⚠ Non-toxic ☆ Electronic electrons

Tantalum is found in the same ores as niobium. It is used to make capacitors and resistors, important electronic components found in almost every mobile phone, laptop, and tablet. Demand is so high that some say we might run out in just 50 years—a good reason to recycle old electronic gadgets.

FIND IT IN:

☐ MOBILE PHONES
☐ LAPTOPS
☐ TABLETS
☐ MOST SMALL ELECTRONIC ITEMS

Tungsten

74 W

◉ Silvery-gray metal
⚠ Non-toxic ☆ Super hard

FIND IT IN:

- ☐ OLD-STYLE LIGHT BULBS
- ☐ MODERN HALOGEN BULBS
- ☐ DRILLS
- ☐ JEWELRY

"Tungsten," a Swedish word meaning "heavy stone," comes from the ore wolframite, hence its code name W. It is similar in density to gold, and has the second highest melting point after carbon.

Drawn into a very fine wire, tungsten was used in the filaments of old-fashioned incandescent light bulbs. They are being replaced by energy-saving bulbs, but "halogen" bulbs still have tungsten filaments.

Rhenium

75 Re

◉ Shiny silvery-gray metal
⚠ Not known to be toxic
☆ Supersonic flight

Rhenium is incredibly rare in the Earth's crust and similar to tungsten in being both incredibly hard and having one of the highest melting points of all the elements. Alloyed with nickel it is used in jet engines, meaning that element detectives can simply listen for the roar of planes flying by!

FIND IT IN:

- ☐ JET PLANES

Osmium

76 Os

◉ Bluish-white metal
⚠ Highly toxic compounds ☆ Life saver

Osmium takes its name from the Greek word for "smell." You'll have a job sniffing it out, though, as it's the rarest stable element in the Earth's crust.

It is also the densest stable element ("stable" meaning it doesn't change over time due to radioactive decay). Osmium resists corrosion, so it is used in the electrical connections in the pacemakers that keep damaged hearts beating correctly and in artificial heart valves. Can you track down anyone kept alive by osmium?

FIND IT IN:

- ☐ PACEMAKERS

Iridium

77 Ir

◉ Shiny white metal ⚠ Low toxicity ☆ Immune to attack

Iridium is so chemically unreactive that chemists are yet to find an acid that will attack it. It is incredibly rare, existing as a thin layer in the Earth's crust from about the time the dinosaurs died out.

FIND IT IN:

- ☐ SPARK PLUGS
- ☐ FOUNTAIN PENS

One theory is that this iridium was part of a meteor or asteroid that hit the Earth, throwing up a dust cloud that led to their extinction. As well as killing dinosaurs, iridium is used in spark plugs, and you might find a tiny blob on the tip of an expensive fountain pen.

Platinum

^{78}Pt

- 👁 Soft gray-white metal
- ⚠ Non-toxic ☆ Super converter

The name for platinum comes from a Spanish word meaning "little silver." In the Earth's crust it is almost as rare as gold, and the metals are often found together. They are both very expensive. Platinum is highly ductile and is often used for fine jewelry, special collectible coins, and even ceremonial crowns.

FIND IT IN:

- ☐ JEWELRY
- ☐ SPECIAL COINS AND MEDALLIONS
- ☐ CROWNS
- ☐ CATALYTIC CONVERTERS...

Britain's Crown Jewels include one crown made entirely from platinum (Pt) and 2,800 diamonds (C).

🔍 Check the cat

If you want to track down this element, try looking in the car. Platinum is an important component of catalytic converters in car exhaust systems. Because of its value, platinum is usually removed and recycled when cars are scrapped.

Gold

^{79}Au

- 👁 Soft shiny yellow metal
- ⚠ Non-toxic
- ☆ Shape changer

Gold is the noblest of the noble metals, being very unreactive and occurring naturally as grains, veins, and nuggets all over the world. But it is very rare, and its scarcity along with its beauty create its high value.

Because it doesn't corrode in water or react with air like other metals it stays shiny forever—just think of all the gleaming treasures of ancient Egypt.

The gold in the Earth's crust is thought to have been brought here by asteroids that crashed onto the planet some 4 billion years ago, close to the time when life first arose. Gold can be found in veins associated with quartz and other minerals as well as in a mixture with silver known as electrum. Sometimes very lucky people just come across nuggets. So keep your eyes peeled!

All at sea

Seawater contains gold, but you will have trouble detecting it. To recover just one gram of gold, you would need the equivalent of 400 Olympic swimming pools of seawater.

FIND IT IN:

- ☐ JEWELRY
- ☐ LUXURY FOODS
- ☐ ELECTRONIC DEVICES
- ☐ SEAWATER
- ☐ FOOD ADDITIVE, E175

silver   gold   platinum

Gold calling

Gold doesn't corrode and is a great conductor of electricity, so tiny amounts are used for electrical connections in computers and mobile phones. Some experts reckon you could recover 1g of gold by recycling just 40 mobile phones. That's easier than sifting 400 swimming pools of seawater!

What a softie

Gold is a very soft metal. It is highly "ductile" and can be pulled into a wire just one atom thick! It is also the most malleable metal, meaning it is easily reshaped. A single gram of gold can be beaten into an incredibly thin sheet that is an amazing 1 meter square. Thin sheets called "gold leaf" are used to decorate books, furniture, and ornaments. The leaf can be made so thin that it is no more than 400 to 500 atoms thick. Because gold is non-toxic, gold leaf is safe to eat, so you might find it decorating luxury chocolates.

🔍 The case of the gold stamp

Pure gold is known as 24-karat (24K). This is very soft, so gold is often alloyed with metals such as copper or silver to make jewelry. These alloys are given lower karat ratings (22K, 18K, 9K...). They are harder but contain less gold.

Gold items often carry a stamp known as a hallmark, which indicates the quality of the gold used and where the item was made. To track down some precious metal elements, grab a magnifying glass and examine some jewelry. Different precious metals have different marks, so check them against the secret codes below...

Mercury

80 Hg

👁 Silvery-white liquid
⚠ Toxic ☆ Superfast

Mercury is one of two elements in the Periodic Table that are liquid at room temperature. Spill the liquid metal and it forms shiny little balls that roll so rapidly that mercury is sometimes called "quicksilver." It was known to the ancient Romans as "hydrargyrum," meaning "water-silver," giving us its code name Hg.

Mercury is extracted by roasting a red mineral called cinnabar. Prehistoric people used powdered cinnabar to make cave paintings, without realizing how toxic mercury compounds can be. Renaissance painters also used it in the pigment vermilion, so many old masterpieces are potentially poisonous!

FIND IT IN:

☐ TINNED FISH

☐ OLD THERMOMETERS AND BAROMETERS

☐ MERCURY VAPOR STREET LIGHTS

Something fishy

Mercury was used in thermometers until people realized the danger of sucking a breakable glass tube containing a toxic element. Dental fillings also contained mercury, but these are being replaced by safer resins. Today, mercury is almost absent from our homes, but you might track it down in tinned fish. Shark, swordfish, marlin, and tuna accumulate mercury by eating smaller fish which have been feeding on smaller organisms containing the element. Stay safe by not eating the riskiest fish too often.

Thallium

^{81}Tl

👁 Soft silvery metal
⚠ Highly toxic ☆ Secret poisoner

Thallium is very easily absorbed by plants and animals, and we probably all contain tiny traces of it (but not enough to harm us). You can track it down in pine trees, which seem particularly good at accumulating it—with up to 100 parts per million.

Where there's a will...

Thallium and its salts are all highly poisonous, and thallium sulfate (Tl_2SO_4) was once a popular rat poison. As it is tasteless and odorless, it was popular with murderers for killing rich relatives—earning it the nickname "inheritance powder."

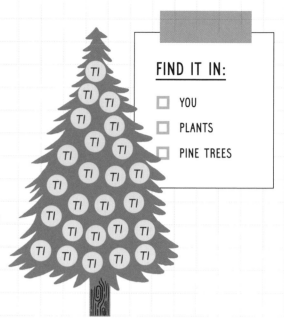

FIND IT IN:

☐ YOU

☐ PLANTS

☐ PINE TREES

Lead

^{82}Pb

👁 Soft, dense, gray metal
⚠ Toxic ☆ Waterproof

The ancient Romans made lead into pipes to carry water in cities across their empire. The Latin word for lead, "plumbum," gives us its code name Pb, and our modern word "plumbing." Copper and plastic have replaced it today, as lead is now known to be toxic, but you may still track it down in the plumbing of old houses. Lead flashing is also used on roofs to keep the rain out.

FIND IT IN:

☐ OLD GRANDFATHER CLOCKS

☐ OLD PLUMBING PIPES

☐ LEAD FLASHING ON ROOFS

☐ CAR BATTERIES

☐ CAR WHEEL BALANCE WEIGHTS

☐ SOLDER IN ELECTRICAL COMPONENTS

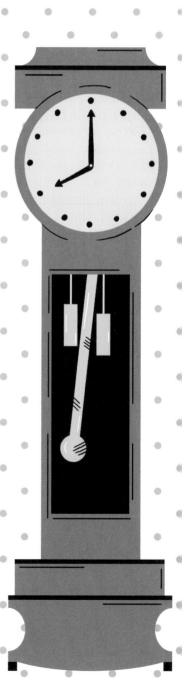

Heavy metal

Lead is one of the densest stable elements, so you might find it in the weights of an old grandfather clock. It can be easily melted and molded, so anglers sometimes use small lead weights to sink their lines, but these are banned in some countries because they can poison waterfowl. In the past, a lead additive called tetraethyl lead was added to gasoline to help engines run smoothly. This was emitted in poisonous exhaust fumes, which is why we now use *un*leaded gas.

Take the lead

While lead is no longer added to fuel, most cars still rely on it to run. Most of the world's supply goes into making lead-acid batteries for cars, and lead weights are attached to car wheels to make them turn evenly. Some lead is added to glass to make expensive lead-crystal tableware. It can also be a component in pewter crockery and the solder used for electrical connections. However, because lead is so toxic, people will keep working on ways to replace it.

IN THE LATE 1800S, MOST PEOPLE STILL AGREED WITH ANCIENT GREEK DEMOCRITUS (C. 460 – C. 370 BCE) THAT ATOMS WERE THE SMALLEST PARTICLES POSSIBLE...

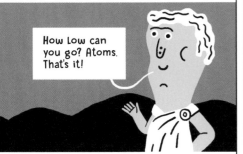

How low can you go? Atoms. That's it!

BUT NEW EVIDENCE WAS EMERGING...

IN 1895, GERMAN PHYSICIST WILHELM RÖNTGEN DISCOVERED X–RAYS – INVISIBLE RAYS PRODUCED BY A HIGH VOLTAGE ELECTRICAL DISCHARGE TUBE...

I deserve a big hand – like this one here!

CALLED "X" FOR "UNKNOWN" AS HE DIDN'T KNOW WHAT THEY WERE.

A YEAR LATER, FRENCH PHYSICIST HENRI BECQUEREL FOUND THAT A MINERAL CALLED PITCHBLENDE* ALSO GAVE OFF INVISIBLE RAYS THAT FOGGED PHOTOGRAPHIC PAPER...

It needs no electricity. How does it do it?

*NOW KNOWN AS URANINITE.

PITCHBLENDE WAS KNOWN TO CONTAIN URANIUM, AN ELEMENT DISCOVERED 100 YEARS EARLIER BY GERMAN CHEMIST MARTIN KLAPROTH...

I named it after Uranus.

Charming!

URANIUM = U. BUT WAS THAT ALL IT CONTAINED?

BECQUEREL'S WORK INTERESTED MARIE CURIE, A PHYSICIST BORN IN POLAND AND MARRIED TO ANOTHER GREAT PHYSICIST, FRENCHMAN PIERRE CURIE...

I ♥ U

MARIE CURIE, BORN POLAND, 1867: DIED FRANCE, 1934
PIERRE CURIE, BORN FRANCE, 1859: DIED FRANCE, 1906

MARIE REALIZED THAT THERE WAS SOMETHING SPECIAL ABOUT URANIUM...

The rays must come from within the atoms. Perhaps atoms can be divided!

THIS WAS A BREAKTHROUGH IN ATOMIC THEORY.

HOWEVER, WHEN SHE COMPARED PURE URANIUM TO PITCHBLENDE, SHE FOUND THAT THE MINERAL PRODUCED FAR MORE INVISIBLE RADIATION...

I think there's something else active in there!

SHE WAS RIGHT!

IN JULY 1898, AFTER PROCESSING TONS OF PITCHBLENDE, THE TWO CURIES ANNOUNCED THE EXISTENCE OF A NEW ELEMENT EVEN MORE ACTIVE THAN URANIUM...

We call it polonium...

After my native country of Poland!

BUT THAT WASN'T ALL...

JUST FIVE MONTHS LATER, THEY FOUND YET ANOTHER ELEMENT IN PITCHBLENDE...

We call it radium...

And it's even more radioactive!*

*THE CURIES COINED THE TERM "RADIOACTIVITY."

IN 1903, PIERRE AND MARIE ALONG WITH HENRI BECQUEREL WERE AWARDED THE NOBEL PRIZE IN PHYSICS FOR THEIR JOINT WORK ON RADIATION.

MARIE WAS THE FIRST WOMAN EVER TO WIN A NOBEL PRIZE!

SADLY PIERRE DIED IN A ROAD ACCIDENT IN 1906, LEAVING MARIE TO WORK ON ALONE. IN 1910, SHE FINALLY ISOLATED PURE RADIUM, AND IN 1911...

I've won another Nobel Prize, this time for chemistry, and all by myself!

MARIE IS THE ONLY PERSON TO HAVE WON NOBEL PRIZES IN TWO DIFFERENT SCIENCES, AND REMAINS THE ONLY WOMAN TO HAVE WON ONE TWICE.

MARIE DIED IN 1934, NOT HAVING REALIZED HOW DANGEROUS RADIUM WAS. HER OLD LABORATORY NOTEBOOKS ARE STILL SO HIGHLY RADIOACTIVE THEY ARE KEPT IN LEAD BOXES AND READ WHILE WEARING PROTECTIVE CLOTHING...

At least you can read them in the dark...

THE CURIES HAVE AN ELEMENT NAMED AFTER THEM. CAN YOU FIND IT?

Bismuth

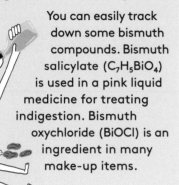

^{83}Bi

◉ Pink-tinged silvery metal
⚠ Thought safe ☆ Tummy tamer

You can easily track down some bismuth compounds. Bismuth salicylate ($C_7H_5BiO_4$) is used in a pink liquid medicine for treating indigestion. Bismuth oxychloride (BiOCl) is an ingredient in many make-up items.

HOT WINGS

FIND IT IN:

- ☐ PINK STOMACH MEDICINE
- ☐ EYE SHADOW
- ☐ PEARL EFFECT NAIL POLISH
- ☐ FACE POWDER

Polonium

^{84}Po

◉ Soft silvery metal ⚠ Lethal
☆ Radioactive killer

Polonium marks the start of the "unstable table." It is so radioactive that you could be killed by less than a single microgram—equivalent to one five-hundredth of the mass of a single grain of salt. All its isotopes have short half-lives, so it doesn't stay around for long.

FIND IT IN:

- ☐ TOBACCO SMO[KE] (AVOID!)
- ☐ THE NATURAL WORLD (IN TIN[Y] AMOUNTS)

Astatine

^{85}At

◉ Unknown, probably a dark non-metal ⚠ Lethal ☆ Super rare

The name means "unstable" and astatine is exactly that. All its isotopes are radioactive and decay into bismuth or polonium in about eight hours. Astatine exists in nature—from the radioactive decay of uranium—but scientists estimate that at any one moment there is never more than 25g of astatine on the planet.

FIND IT IN:

- ☐ ATOMIC LABORATORIES
- ☐ THE NATURAL WORLD (IN TINY AMOUNTS)

Radon

^{86}Rn

◉ Colorless, odorless gas
⚠ Lethal ☆ Invisibility

Radon is a member of the noble gases, but a dodgy customer best avoided. It is produced naturally from rocks containing uranium and thorium, especially in areas with a lot of granite. The invisible gas leaks out of the ground and collects in the basements of houses, radon being the densest gas at room temperature. It is responsible for half the nuclear radiation we are exposed to daily.

FIND IT IN:

- ☐ AIR
- ☐ GRANITE
- ☐ SOME SOILS

Francium

^{87}Fr

◉ Unknown, probably a silvery metal
⚠ Lethal ☆ Radioactive

Francium is the second rarest element in the Earth's crust after astatine and has a half-life of just 22 minutes. What little exists is mostly made in nuclear reactors, although a New York university once managed to create as many as ten thousand atoms. (That may sound impressive, but one grain of table salt contains about 1.2 billion billion atoms!)

FIND IT IN:

- ☐ NUCLEAR REACTORS

Radium

^{88}R[a]

◉ Silvery-white metal
⚠ Lethal ☆ Radioactive

Radium was once thought to be good for us and was added to mineral water, make-up, toothpaste, bathwater, and even chocolate. Mixtures of radium and phosphorescent chemicals were also painted on "luminous" watch dials so they could be read in the dark. We know now it is highly dangerous.

FIND IT IN:

- ☐ OLD "LUMINOUS" CLOCKS A[ND] WATCHES
- ☐ GRANITE ROCKS

ONE SCIENTIST DID MORE THAN ANY OTHER TO UNLOCK THE SECRETS OF THE ATOM AND RADIOACTIVITY...

I certainly had a full life, not a half-life...

HIS NAME WAS ERNEST RUTHERFORD. BORN NEW ZEALAND, 1871; DIED UK, 1937

THE SON OF A FARMER, THE YOUNG ERNEST WAS SUPER-GOOD AT SCIENCE AND EVENTUALLY ENDED UP AT ONE OF THE WORLD'S LEADING RESEARCH ESTABLISHMENTS...

Here at Last!

(THE CAVENDISH LABORATORY AT THE UNIVERSITY OF CAMBRIDGE. ENGLAND.)

HIS BOSS WAS THE GREAT PHYSICIST J.J. THOMSON, WHO IN 1897 DISCOVERED THE FIRST SUB-ATOMIC PARTICLE, THE ELECTRON.

Guilty as charged!

PEOPLE BEGAN TO REALIZE ATOMS MIGHT BE MADE UP OF SMALLER THINGS.

THOMSON THOUGHT THAT ELECTRONS WERE DISTRIBUTED INSIDE A SPHERE OF POSITIVE CHARGE, FORMING ATOMS.

I call it my "plum pudding" theory.

Delicious!

HOWEVER, THIS WASN'T QUITE RIGHT—AS RUTHERFORD WOULD LATER SHOW.

MEANWHILE, ERNEST WENT TO CANADA, WHERE HE DISCOVERED THAT THE ELEMENT URANIUM EMITTED TWO PREVIOUSLY UNKNOWN TYPES OF RADIATION.

I shall call them alpha-rays and beta-rays!

(AFTER THE FIRST TWO LETTERS OF THE GREEK ALPHABET, OF COURSE...)

WORKING WITH CHEMIST FREDERICK SODDY, THE TWO MEN CAME UP WITH THE RADICAL IDEA THAT ATOMS COULD ACTUALLY CHANGE, RELEASING RADIATION IN THE PROCESS.

Atoms aren't indestructible!

Democritus was wrong!

AND IT ONLY TOOK SCIENCE 2,000 YEARS TO PROVE IT!

RUTHERFORD THEN IDENTIFIED A THIRD TYPE OF HIGHLY PENETRATING RADIATION, THIS TIME EMITTED BY RADIUM.

And guess what I called it...

(GAMMA—FROM THE THIRD LETTER OF THE GREEK ALPHABET.)

BUSY OLD RUTHERFORD THEN RETURNED TO THE UK, WHERE IN 1907 HE SHOWED THAT ALPHA-RAYS WERE ACTUALLY HELIUM ATOMS MINUS THEIR ELECTRONS. THIS WAS ANOTHER BREAKTHROUGH.

One element can produce another!

α

AND RUTHERFORD HAD A FURTHER SUSPICION...

AFTER WINNING THE NOBEL PRIZE IN 1908, HE SET ABOUT BOMBARDING A THIN GOLD FOIL WITH ALPHA PARTICLES. MOST PASSED STRAIGHT THROUGH, BUT A FEW WERE DEFLECTED AS IF THEY HAD HIT SOMETHING.

I think I've hit on something too!

RUTHERFORD HAD POLISHED OFF THE "PLUM PUDDING" THEORY!

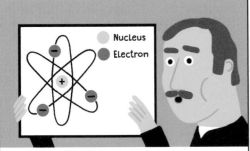

RUTHERFORD BELIEVED ATOMS WERE MOSTLY SPACE WITH ELECTRONS ORBITING A SMALL CONCENTRATED NUCLEUS.

Nucleus
Electron

BUT WHAT MADE UP A NUCLEUS?

IN 1920, RUTHERFORD SUGGESTED THAT HYDROGEN NUCLEI WERE POSITIVELY CHARGED PARTICLES WHICH HE CALLED PROTONS, AND IN 1932 ONE OF HIS COLLEAGUES, JAMES CHADWICK, DISCOVERED THE NEUTRON.

Earning me the nickname "Jimmy Neutron"!

JAMES CHADWICK, BORN UK, 1891; DIED UK, 1974

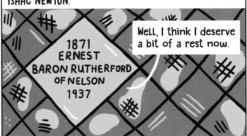

RUTHERFORD IS KNOWN AS THE FATHER OF NUCLEAR PHYSICS. HE DIED IN 1937 AND HIS ASHES WERE BURIED IN WESTMINSTER ABBEY, CLOSE TO THE GREAT SIR ISAAC NEWTON.

1871 ERNEST BARON RUTHERFORD OF NELSON 1937

Well, I think I deserve a bit of a rest now.

IN 1997, A NEW ELEMENT WAS NAMED AFTER HIM. CAN YOU FIND IT ON THE TABLE?

THE LANTHANIDES

The Periodic Table contains two secret doors to new rows of elements, grouped below the main table. The first row comes after barium and contains the elements with atomic numbers from 57 to 71. These are the lanthanides.

Find it in

Lanthanum
57 La

◉ Soft silvery-white metal
⚠ Moderately toxic ☆ Micro camera

Lanthanum is increasingly important in our high-tech world. Added to glass, it allows camera lenses to be made small enough to fit your mobile phone and plays a role in rechargeable batteries used in laptops.

📍 CAMERA PHONE LENSES, LAPTOP BATTERIES, HYBRID CAR BATTERIES

58 Ce Cerium

◉ Soft gray metal ⚠ Non-toxic ☆ Super inventor

You can track down cerium compounds in flat-screen TVs and low-energy light bulbs. Cerium oxide (CeO_2) coats self-cleaning oven interiors. Cerium sulfide (Ce_2S_3) is used to make safe red and yellow paints for toys.

📍 FLAT-SCREEN TVS, LOW-ENERGY BULBS, LIGHTER FLINTS, CATALYTIC CONVERTERS, SELF-CLEANING OVENS, TOYS

Praseodymium
59 Pr

◉ Soft silvery metal ⚠ Low toxicity
☆ Super light filter

Added to glass, praseodymium filters out infrared light, the sort of radiation we feel as heat. So it is added, with neodymium, to the glass safety goggles of welders and glassblowers.

📍 LIGHTER FLINTS, YELLOW CUBIC ZIRCONIA JEWELRY

Neodymium
60 Nd

◉ Silvery-white metal
⚠ Moderately toxic ☆ Super magnetic

Added to iron along with boron, neodymium produces magnets so strong that even tiny ones can be effective. You might find these in earphones or the speaker of your smartphone. It also gives glass a purple tint.

📍 EARPHONES, SMARTPHONE SPEAKERS, PURPLE GLASS

Promethium
61 Pm

◉ Silvery metal ⚠ Radioactive ☆ Mysterious

Promethium is a mystery metal. Unusually for a lanthanide it is radioactive. It can be made in laboratories and its salts have a pink tinge that gives off a greenish glow. It releases "beta particles"—high-energy electrons that are sometimes used in factory devices for checking the thickness of fabrics.

📍 RESEARCH LABORATORIES, SOME PAPER MAY HAVE BEEN EXPOSED TO IT

62 Sm Samarium

◉ Silvery metal ⚠ Slightly toxic ☆ Super magnetic

Samarium, like neodymium, makes magnets 10,000 times as strong as plain iron ones. These turn up in luxury headphones, MP3 players, and "noiseless" pick-ups on electric guitars, which turn vibrations into electrical signals.

📍 HEADPHONES, MP3 PLAYERS, IPODS, ELECTRIC GUITAR PICK-UPS

63 Eu Europium

◉ Soft silvery metal ⚠ Slightly toxic
☆ Anti-faker

Europium hides in the ink used to print Euro banknotes, making them harder to forge. The europium glows red or blue (depending on the compound) under UV light.

📍 EURO NOTES, OLD TV SCREENS, LOW-ENERGY LIGHT BULBS

64 Gd Gadolinium

- 👁 Silvery-white metal
- ⚠ Moderately toxic ☆ Super scanner

Gadolinium has an important role in high-tech healthcare equipment, including MRI scanners that are used to look inside our bodies.

📍 MRI SCANNERS, GREEN TV PHOSPHORS

Terbium 65 Tb

- 👁 Soft silvery metal
- ⚠ Slightly toxic ☆ Light giver

Terbium is named after the Ytterby mine in Sweden, where many elements have been discovered in minerals. It is used to give a green light in low-energy bulbs, which mixes with red and blue to create white light.

📍 ENERGY-SAVING BULBS

Dysprosium 66 Dy

- 👁 Soft silvery metal ⚠ Slightly toxic
- ☆ Wind generator

Some dysprosium is used in nuclear power stations, in the rods that control the reactor's temperature. Wind turbines also have iron-dysprosium alloy magnets that can withstand great heat.

📍 NUCLEAR POWER STATIONS, WIND TURBINES

Holmium 67 Ho

- 👁 Soft silvery metal ⚠ Non-toxic ☆ Colorful

Holmium has few uses outside of nuclear reactors, even though it's 20 times more abundant in the Earth's crust than silver. Holmium oxide (Ho_2O_3) gives a red or yellow tinge to glass and cubic zirconia jewelry.

📍 CUBIC ZIRCONIA JEWELRY, GLASS, NUCLEAR REACTORS

68 Er Erbium

- 👁 Soft silvery metal ⚠ Mildly toxic
- ☆ Super broadband

Erbium is also named for the Ytterby mine. It is used in nuclear power station control rods to absorb neutrons and keep things safe. Erbium oxide (Er_2O_3) imparts a pink hue to jewelry, and also soups up fiber-optic cables.

📍 NUCLEAR POWER STATIONS, FIBER-OPTIC CABLES, PINK CUBIC ZIRCONIA

Thulium 69 Tm

- 👁 Silvery-gray metal ⚠ Non-toxic ☆ X-ray vision

Thulium is used as a source of X-rays in portable X-ray machines employed in emergencies outdoors. It also glows green under UV light and is another rare earth element you can discover printed on Euros.

📍 EURO BANKNOTES, X-RAY MACHINES

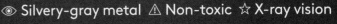

Ytterbium 70 Yb

- 👁 Soft silvery metal ⚠ Slightly toxic ☆ Unknown

Guess where the name comes from! Outside of research laboratories, ytterbium has very few uses. So if you really want to track some down, you'll have to become a super-scientist—or visit Ytterby village in Sweden!

📍 SCIENTIFIC LABORATORIES, YTTERBY

71 Lu Lutetium

- 👁 Hard silvery metal ⚠ Slightly toxic
- ☆ Meteoric measurer

Lutetium mostly haunts science labs, though it has some special medical uses. One of its isotopes, 176-Lu, has a half-life of about 38 billion years and is used to date meteorites!

📍 SCIENTIFIC LABORATORIES, METEORITES

ATOMIC COMICS
THE MANHATTAN PROJECT DETECTIVES:
THE CASE OF THE ATOMIC BOMB

AS YOU KNOW, IN THE PAST MANY NATURALLY OCCURRING ELEMENTS WERE DISCOVERED ACCIDENTALLY BY THE ANCIENTS...

Ooh!

SOME WERE DISCOVERED ACCIDENTALLY BY ALCHEMISTS...

Ooh!

AND LOTS WERE DISCOVERED ON PURPOSE BY SIR HUMPHRY DAVY...

I found seven. Arr!

PLUS OTHER GREAT CHEMISTS TOO, OF COURSE...

SINCE THE BIRTH OF NUCLEAR PHYSIC MANY MANMADE ELEMENTS HAVE BE SYNTHESIZED BY COMBINING PARTICL AS WELL AS PULLING THEM APART...

Smashing atoms?

Yes, they ar rather lovel

*SEE ATOMIC COMIC #9.

THIS RELEASED AN ENORMOUS AMOUNT OF ENERGY, CALCULATED ACCORDING TO THE MOST FAMOUS EQUATION IN SCIENCE, $E = MC^2$ (SQUARED).

Formulated by me, the great genius* Albert Einstein!

BORN GERMANY, 1879: DIED USA, 1955
*MAD HAIR, THOUGH.

OTTO HAHN WAS GIVEN THE 1944 NOBEL PRIZE FOR CHEMISTRY FOR THEIR WORK – BUT NOT LISE MEITNER! TO MANY THIS SEEMED VERY UNFAIR.

Otto was a great chemist, but he doesn't have an element named after him. I do!

CAN YOU FIND IT?

SCIENTISTS REALIZED NUCLEAR FISSION COULD BE USED TO BUILD AN ATOMIC BOMB. AS WORLD WAR 2 RAGED, THE ALLIES* RUSHED TO SUCCEED BEFORE ADOLF HITLER'S NAZI GERMANY. THEIR TOP SECRET MISSION WAS CALLED...

The Manhattan Project, Shh!

*USA, UK, AND CANADA.

THE PROJECT ATTRACTED SOME OF TH GREATEST NUCLEAR SCIENTISTS OF TH DAY. THESE INCLUDED EDWIN MCMILLA

In 1940, I made the first ever transuranic element—"element 93"—now known as neptunium*.

BORN USA, 1907: DIED USA 1991
*AFTER THE PLANET NEPTUNE.
SEE PAGE 58.

PRODUCING PLUTONIUM WAS A MAJOR PART OF THE MANHATTAN PROJECT. IT FUELED THE BOMB DROPPED ON THE JAPANESE CITY OF NAGASAKI ON AUGUST 9TH, 1945.

IT ENDED THE WAR WITH JAPAN, BUT KILLED OVER 70,000 PEOPLE – MOST OF THEM CIVILIANS.

IT REMAINS THE LAST TIME A NUCLEAR WEAPON WAS USED IN A CONFLICT...SO FAR.

ANOTHER TOP PHYSICIST ON THE TEAM WAS ALBERT GHIORSO...

You can call me Al.

BORN USA, 1915: DIED USA, 2010

ALONG WITH SEABORG, THE PAIR CREA TWO MORE NEW ELEMENTS*, BUT HAD KEEP THEM SECRET BECAUSE OF THE W

*AMERICIUM (95) AND CURIUM (96). (! PAGES 58–59.)

SIX OF GHIORSO'S ELEMENTS ARE NAMED AFTER OTHER GREAT SCIENTISTS:

It's me again!

(ERNEST RUTHERFORD, GLENN SEABORG, DMITRI MENDELEEV, ENRICO FERMI, ALBERT EINSTEIN, ERNEST LAWRENCE)

NEW ELEMENTS ARE STILL BEING CREATED AROUND THE WORLD. SOMETIMES ONLY A FEW ATOMS EXIST AND LAST FOR LESS THAN A SECOND...

Where's it gone?

LIVERMORIUM (116) HAS A HALF-LIFE OF JUST 60 MILLISECONDS!

NEW DISCOVERIES HAVE TO BE CONFIRMED BY THE INTERNATIONAL UNION OF PURE AND APPLIED CHEMISTRY BASED IN ZURICH AND CHICAGO...

IUPAC

LUCKILY KNOWN AS IUPAC, FOR SHORT.

THEY ALSO DECIDE WHAT NAME A NEW ELEMENT WILL HAVE...

Can I call it Fred? Eric? Agatha? Bimbleshanks?

Non.

10

RIAN–SWEDISH PHYSICIST LISE
NER AND GERMAN CHEMIST OTTO
N WERE THE FIRST TO SPLIT AN ATOM.

We split it...

Together!

MEITNER, 1878–1968;
HAHN, 1879–1968

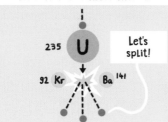

IN 1938, WITH THE SUPPORT OF MEITNER,
HAHN FIRED NEUTRONS AT URANIUM ATOMS.
A URANIUM NUCLEUS ABSORBED A NEUTRON
TO SPLIT INTO TWO SMALLER ATOMS...

235 U

Let's split!

92 Kr   Ba 141

A PROCESS WE NOW CALL NUCLEAR
FISSION.

D DR GLENN T. SEABORG.

"Seaborg."
not "cyborg!"

USA, 1912; DIED USA, 1999

IN 1940, ALONG WITH MCMILLAN
AND OTHERS, SEABORG SUCCESSFULLY
BOMBARDED URANIUM WITH HIGH-
SPEED HYDROGEN NUCLEI TO CREATE
NEW ELEMENT 94...

We call it "plutonium" after Pluto.

Woof!*

*NOT THE DOG, THE PLANET!

AFTER IT ENDED THERE WAS NO
PING THEM...

-discovered 10 new elements!

And I
co-
discovered
a dozen!

THEM ALL ON PAGES 58 TO 60!

TO DATE, ALBERT GHIORSO HOLDS THE
RECORD FOR HAVING DISCOVERED THE
GREATEST NUMBER OF ELEMENTS.

I admit
defeat. Arr!

| DAVY | 7 |
| GHIORSO | 12 |

Y, THE GREATEST LIVING ELEMENT
ER IS YURI OGANESSIAN OF
JOINT INSTITUTE FOR NUCLEAR
RCH IN DUBNA, RUSSIA.

far I have
iscovered five!

Ha! Beat you! Arr!

IS THE ONLY PERSON ALIVE WITH
LEMENT NAMED AFTER THEM.
YOU FIND IT?

NO DOUBT YET MORE ELEMENTS WILL
CONTINUE TO BE CREATED. MAYBE ONE
DAY, YOU MIGHT DISCOVER ONE! BUT
WHAT WOULD YOU CALL IT?

8
Og
GANESSON

—
YOUR-NAME-
HERE-IUM
—

GOOD LUCK!

Splitting the atom

Elements not found in nature but made artificially in laboratories are called "synthetic." They include americium and all those beyond it in the table. They are all unstable: their nuclei change ("decay"), producing potentially harmful radioactivity which can be detected with special equipment such as a Geiger counter.

Intriguing isotopes

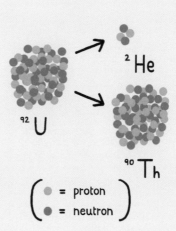

^{2}He

^{90}Th

^{92}U

(● = proton)
(● = neutron)

Atoms with the same number of protons but different numbers of neutrons are called isotopes. Uranium has several isotopes all with 92 protons but with between 140 and 146 neutrons in their nuclei. Uranium-235 has 143 neutrons, but its unstable nuclei decay by emitting radioactive alpha particles consisting of two protons and two neutrons. By losing two protons, uranium (92) becomes thorium (90)—a dangerous change of identity!

The three suspects

There are three types of radiation produced by the nuclei of radioactive elements. All can cause harm by damaging the cells and processes of living things through the creation of ions (see page 9). All three are best avoided!

α alpha

β beta

γ gamma

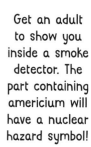

Get an adult to show you inside a smoke detector. The part containing americium will have a nuclear hazard symbol!

🔍 The case of the alarming alpha particles

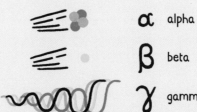

All homes should have smoke detectors to warn us if a fire has started. They contain a tiny amount of radioactive americium (see page 58). Americium atoms constantly decay to emit alpha particles that cross a small gap inside the alarm and maintain an electrical circuit. Smoke entering the detector interferes with the alpha particles, breaking the circuit and triggering the alarm.

THE ACTINIDES

The second secret door in the Periodic Table reveals the row after radium, with atomic numbers (the number of protons) increasing from 89 to 103. These are the actinides. They are all radioactive and potentially harmful.

📍 Find it in

Actinium

89 Ac

👁 Soft silvery-white metal
⚠ Radioactive ☆ Glow in the dark

Tiny traces of actinium are produced by the radioactive decay of uranium ores. Actinium emits alpha particles, which ionize the air and give the element a pale-blue glow. Highly dangerous, but not found in homes. Phew!

📍 NUCLEAR REACTORS, LABORATORIES

Thorium

90 Th

👁 Soft silvery metal
⚠ Weakly radioactive ☆ Light giver

Radioactive thorium is best avoided, but thorium oxide (ThO_2) is used in gas camping lamp mantles. These are cloth bags placed over the burners that glow with a bright white light.

📍 SOIL, CAMPING LAMPS, GRANITE KITCHEN WORKTOPS

Protactinium

91 Pa

👁 Dense silvery metal
⚠ Highly radioactive ☆ Unknown

Protactinium decays into actinium, hence its name, which comes from a Greek word meaning "first" or "before" actinium. What protactinium there is—and there isn't much—has no known uses.

📍 URANIUM ORES, NUCLEAR REACTORS

Uranium

92 U

👁 Silvery metal ⚠ Radioactive ☆ Devastation

The ancient Romans, knowing nothing about radioactivity, used radioactive uranium salts to color glass a pretty yellow. And as recently as the 1940s a US company used uranium oxide to color Fiestaware crockery a brilliant red. Now it's used in reactors and weapons.

📍 ROMAN GLASSWARE, ANTIQUE FIESTAWARE POTTERY, NUCLEAR REACTORS...

Neptunium

93 Np

👁 Silvery metal ⚠ Radioactive ☆ Element maker

Neptunium is the first "transuranic" element—a term for all those elements beyond uranium in the Periodic Table. All are unstable and radioactive. Neptunium is made in laboratories and nuclear reactors and is used to make other transuranic elements.

📍 NUCLEAR REACTORS, LABORATORIES

Plutonium

94 Pu

👁 Silvery metal ⚠ Highly radioactive ☆ Space travel

Third in the line of elements named after planets, plutonium is made by bombarding uranium with neutrons in nuclear reactors and will be around as hazardous waste for tens of thousands of years.

📍 NUCLEAR REACTORS, LABORATORIES

Americium

95 Am

👁 Silvery metal ⚠ Radioactive ☆ Smoke signals

Americium was first created in 1944 by US matter-maker Glenn T. Seaborg. Today it is extracted in small amounts from nuclear reactors, making it both dangerous and expensive. But its best-known use helps keep us safe (see page 57).

📍 NUCLEAR REACTORS, NUCLEAR WEAPONS, SMOKE DETECTORS

Curium

⁹⁶Cm

◉ Silvery metal ⚠ Radioactive ☆ Space travel

Named in honor of Pierre and Marie Curie, only a few grams are made each year, usually inside nuclear reactors. Curium has been used to power spacecraft, so element detectives should look to the stars!

📍 NUCLEAR REACTORS, SPACECRAFT

Berkelium

⁹⁷Bk

◉ Silvery-white metal
⚠ Highly radioactive ☆ Heavy metal maker

Berkelium is named after Berkeley, California, home to the University of California Radiation Laboratory. Just over 1g of this metal has been made in the past 50 years. It is used in research and to make heavier elements.

📍 A CALIFORNIAN LABORATORY

Californium

⁹⁸Cf

◉ Soft silvery metal ⚠ Radioactive
☆ Neutron maker

Californium takes its name from the same location as berkelium. Tiny amounts are made in laboratories and nuclear reactors, and are used as a source of neutrons, sometimes for making other synthetic elements.

📍 LABORATORIES, NUCLEAR REACTORS

Einsteinium

⁹⁹Es

◉ Soft silvery metal
⚠ Radioactive ☆ Reactionary genius

Some einsteinium was detected in the fallout from the first ever hydrogen bomb test back in 1952. Ironically, it is named after genius physicist Albert Einstein, who opposed nuclear weapons.

📍 NUCLEAR REACTORS

Fermium

¹⁰⁰Fm

◉ Silvery metal ⚠ Radioactive ☆ Super rare

Named after Manhattan Project nerd Enrico Fermi. Less than a millionth of a gram is made each year in labs and nuclear reactors. It is the last of the transuranic elements to be made in sufficient quantities to be seen with the naked eye.

📍 NUCLEAR REACTORS, LABORATORIES

Mendelevium

¹⁰¹Md

◉ Unknown ⚠ Radioactive ☆ Mysterious

Named after Dmitri Mendeleev, not enough mendelevium has ever been made to allow it to be seen. Surprisingly, it was named after a Russian chemist by its American discoverers at a time when the USA and the former Soviet Union were fierce rivals.

📍 NO CHANCE

Nobelium

¹⁰²No

◉ Unknown ⚠ Radioactive ☆ Disappearing act

Nobelium is named after Alfred Nobel, instigator of the Nobel Prize. Only a few atoms have ever been made, and even the most stable isotope has a half-life of under an hour. It exists only in laboratories.

📍 NUCLEAR LABORATORIES

Lawrencium

¹⁰³Lr

◉ Unknown ⚠ Radioactive ☆ Super rare

Lawrencium is named after Ernest Lawrence, the American physicist who won the Nobel Prize for inventing the cyclotron particle accelerator. Hardly any atoms have ever been made.

📍 ATOMIC LABORATORIES

The end of the line

After lawrencium, we element detectives must return to the table for a final row of really large atoms, all unstable and highly radioactive. They begin with rutherfordium (atomic number 104) and end—well, who can say? Why should they ever end when clever scientists can continue to smash particles together to produce heavier and heavier atoms? To date, oganesson is the latest name on the table. Only five atoms of Og have been detected and these had a half-life of less than a millisecond.

Name and symbol	Atomic number	Named after	Year of discovery
rutherfordium Rf	104	New Zealand Physicist Ernest Rutherford	1964
dubnium Db	105	Dubna, home of the Russian JINR laboratories	1968
seaborgium Sg	106	US physicist Glenn T. Seaborg	1974
bohrium Bh	107	Danish physicist Niels Bohr	1981
hassium Hs	108	The German state of Hesse	1984
meitnerium Mt	109	Austrian-Swedish Physicist Lise Meitner	1982
darmstadtium Ds	110	Darmstadt, Germany	1994
roentgenium Rg	111	German physicist Wilhelm Röntgen	1994
copernicium Cn	112	Astronomer Nicolaus Copernicus	1996
nihonium Nh	113	An old name for Japan	2004
flerovium Fl	114	Russian physicist Georgy Flyorov	1998
moscovium Mc	115	Moscow, Russia	2003
livermorium Lv	116	Lawrence Livermore National Laboratory, USA	2000
tennessine Ts	117	Tennessee, USA	2010
oganesson Og	118	Russian nuclear physicist Yuri Oganessian (born 1933)	2006

More new elements will surely be made, even if only for the merest sliver of a fraction of a second. And maybe YOU will be the person who discovers them. Already element 119 has a provisional name and symbol—ununennium, Uue—but just imagine what name it might have one day...

If you could somehow take this book with you into the future, these last pages would probably prove the funniest. A hundred years from now, maybe less, people on this planet might wonder how we knew so little about the universe. The previous pages have all been about the matter we know exists, can observe and, after a few thousand years, are finally starting to understand. However, there's much more to the universe than that...

Scientists calculate that the universe has a mass far greater than can be accounted for by ordinary matter made of the elements. In fact, they believe such matter makes up less than 5% of the universe. That is the equivalent of the area of the Periodic Table shown on this page compared to the area of the whole page itself. The rest is dark matter (about 27%) and dark energy (about 68%).They say "dark" because we can't observe it yet—we can only see the effect it has on objects in the universe.

Dark matter and dark energy are a mystery that perhaps one day YOU will shine a light on... Good luck and happy hunting!

Glossary

Allotropes: Differing forms of the same element, in which atoms are arranged differently. Different allotropes often have very different properties, for example, graphite and diamond (both are forms of carbon).

Alloy: A mixture of two or more different substances, of which one is a metal. For example, brass is an alloy of copper and zinc.

Alpha particle (α): A radioactive particle produced when the nucleus of an atom breaks down. It consists of two protons and two neutrons, and is identical to a helium nucleus. Alpha particles are dangerous to living tissues.

Amino acids: The small chemical building blocks that join together in long chains to make up proteins.

Atom: The smallest possible unit of an element that has all the chemical properties of the element. It consists of a nucleus with protons and neutrons orbited by electrons.

Atomic number: The number of protons contained in a nucleus, giving an element its chemical identity.

Atomic weight: The average mass of an atom of an element, most of which comes from the combination of protons and neutrons in its nucleus.

Beta particle (β): A high-speed, high-energy electron emitted from the nucleus of an atom when a neutron changes into a proton plus an electron. Beta particle radiation can also harm living tissues.

Bond: The attraction between atoms, ions or molecules that holds them together. Bonds can be covalent, in which electrons are shared between atoms, ionic, in which opposing electrical charges between ions form the bond, or metallic bonds, which have positive ions in a free-flowing "sea" of electrons. Hydrogen bonds occur when different parts of individual molecules are attracted to each other.

Caustic: A chemical that burns skin or corrodes other substances with which it comes into contact.

Chemical reaction: A process occurring between two or more chemicals that causes a change involving the formation of one or more different substances. It differs from a physical change, such as melting or freezing, in which a substance remains chemically unaltered.

Chemistry: The science and study of substances. It includes investigating their structure and properties, and the changes they undergo when they react with other substances.

Compound: A substance containing the atoms of two or more different elements chemically combined.

Cosmic ray: High-energy electrically charged particles that travel through space, some striking the Earth's atmosphere.

Dark energy: An as yet unknown form of energy that scientists think contributes to most of the mass of the universe.

Dark matter: A theoretical form of matter—different from ordinary matter—proposed by scientists to help explain the nature of the universe. It is called "dark" because it has not yet been directly observed.

Ductile: The ability of a substance—often a metal—to be pulled out into a wire.

Electron: A subatomic particle with a negative electrical charge (-). In atoms electrons orbit the nucleus and an atom with no overall charge has the same number of electrons as it has protons in its nucleus.

Element: A substance composed only of identical atoms, all with the same atomic number and the same chemical properties.

Flammable: Capable of being set on fire.

Gamma ray (γ): A form of electromagnetic radiation produced when the nucleus of an atom breaks apart. Unlike alpha and beta radiation it is not a particle, but it is also dangerous to life.

Gas: The atoms or molecules of a gas move independently of each other and can expand to fill the space they are in. Air is a mixture of gases.

Inert: Chemically unreactive.

Isotope: Atoms of an element that have identical numbers of protons (atomic number) but different numbers of neutrons.

Liquid: A state of matter in which the molecules or atoms have a fixed volume but can flow to occupy the form of a container.

Malleable: Capable of being beaten or stretched into a different shape, usually applied to metals. Gold is soft and highly malleable.

Metal: The majority of elements in the periodic table are metals. They are usually shiny solids and good conductors of heat and electricity. Mercury is unusual as it is liquid at room temperature.

Molecule: A combination of at least two atoms of a single element or various elements.

Mixture: A substance with two or more components that aren't combined chemically and that can be separated by physical means such as filtering, freezing or evaporation.

Neutron: A subatomic particle found in the nucleus; it has no overall electrical charge. Along with protons, neutrons contribute to the mass of an atom.

Nucleus: The center of an atom, containing protons and neutrons.

Nuclear reaction: A change in the nucleus of an atom, often involving the release of radiation.

Ordinary matter: The matter that we can observe and detect in the universe, including all the elements of the periodic table.

Ore: A naturally occurring material that can be mined and processed to extract valuable or useful substances. For example, bauxite is a type of mineral ore from which aluminum is extracted.

Polymer: A substance composed of lots of repeating smaller molecules joined in a long chain.

Proteins: Large molecules made up of chains of amino acids. They help build and run our bodies, and are essential to all living things; they are found in muscles and fur.

Proton: A subatomic particle found in the nucleus; it has a positive (+) electrical charge. The number of protons in an atom (atomic number) gives it its chemical identity.

Radioactivity: The breakdown of an atom's nucleus, which causes radioactive particles or radiation to be released.

Ultraviolet light: A form of electromagnetic radiation that our eyes cannot detect, unlike visible light. Known as UV for short, it is a component of sunlight that causes skin to burn or tan.

Vitamin: A substance essential in small amounts for healthy living. It comes from the words "**vital mineral**."

ZZZZZZoooom!: Ohms, Ratley, and Hattie off in their spaceship!

Index

With huge thanks to Mr Coe, Adam Bedford,
and a happy birthday to Tim

LAURENCE KING

Published in 2018
by Laurence King Publishing Ltd.
361–373 City Road
London EC1V 1LR
Tel: +4420 7841 6900
Email: enquiries@laurenceking.com
www.laurenceking.com

Reprinted 2019

A catalog record for this book is available
from the British Library.

ISBN: 978-1-78627-178-5

Initial design ideas: Charlie Bolton
Final design concept and layout: Claire Clewley
Copy-editing: Jason Hook
Chemistry consultant: Dan Green

Printed in Italy by L.E.G.O. S.p.A.